ΜΝΕΙΑΣ ΧΑΡΙΝ

HERBERT PIERREPONT HOUGHTON

Professor of Classical Languages
1923-1950

FINDING PEOPLE
IN EARLY GREECE

Photo by Mogens Herman Hansen

The Fordyce W. Mitchel Memorial Lecture Series

The Fordyce W. Mitchel Memorial Lecture Series, sponsored by the Department of History at the University of Missouri–Columbia, began in October 2000. Fordyce Mitchel was Professor of Greek History at the University of Missouri–Columbia until his death in 1986. In addition to his work on fourth-century Greek history and epigraphy, including his much-cited *Lykourgan Athens: 338–322*, Mitchel helped to elevate the ancient history program in the Department of History and to build extensive library resources in that field. The lecture series was made possible by a generous endowment from his widow, Marguerite Mitchel. It provides for a biennial series of lectures on original aspects of Greek history and society, given by a scholar of high international standing. The lectures are then revised for publication by the University of Missouri Press.

FINDING
PEOPLE
IN
EARLY
GREECE

Carol G. Thomas

University of Missouri Press
Columbia and London

Library of Congress Cataloging-in-Publication Data

Thomas, Carol G., 1938–
    Finding people in early Greece / Carol G. Thomas.
        p. cm. — (The Fordyce W. Mitchel Memorial Lecture Series)
    Summary: "Explores the marriage of historically oriented scholar-
ship and scientific developments in the study of preclassical Greek
history. Two figures from preclassical Greece are examined: Jason and
the voyage of the Argo, from the Age of Heroes, and Hesiod, who
lived during the Age of Revolution"—Provided by publisher.
    Includes bibliographical references and index.
    ISBN 0-8262-1577-7 (alk. paper)
    1.   Jason (Greek mythology) 2.   Argonauts (Greek mythology)
3.   Hesiod—Criticism and interpretation.   I.   Title. II.   Series.
    BL820.A8T47 2005
    938'.01—dc22
                                                      2004029231

∞™ This paper meets the requirements of the
American National Standard for Permanence of Paper
for Printed Library Materials, Z39.48, 1984.

Designer: Kristie Lee
Typesetter: Crane Composition, Inc.
Printer and Binder: The Maple-Vail Book Manufacturing Group
Typefaces: Berkeley and Tiepolo

For Cynthia and Robert Carter
Modern Argonauts and True Friends

Contents

ACKNOWLEDGMENTS

It was an honor to be invited to present the Fordyce Mitchel Memorial Lecture Series in September 2002. A debt of gratitude is owed to many members of the University of Missouri: to Mrs. Fordyce Mitchel for establishing this lectureship in honor of her husband; to the Department of History for extending the invitation to offer the lectures, especially Ian Worthington, whose role in my visit was particularly helpful; and to faculty, students, and staff in a wide range of departments who extended hospitality of a truly Homeric nature. For this revised version of those lectures, I am grateful to Beverly Jarrett, director and editor in chief of the University of Missouri Press, and to Jane Lago, managing editor of the press. Their efficiency, enthusiasm, and genuine cordiality to potential authors are the essence of the craft of editing.

The invitation was a tribute to preclassical Greek history—the focus of my own work and an era that, until quite recently, has been regarded as a stepchild of true Greek history. As J. C. Stobart reports in *The Glory That Was Greece: A Survey of Hellenic Culture and Civilization,* "Not all the imaginative reconstructions of poetical professors can really throw much light upon it."[1] To be sure, this is an extreme and early perspective coming in the wake of the first declared discoveries that the so-called age of heroes had an existence in more than myth and legend. Even so, some modern scholars continue to emphasize the absence of evidence necessary for full historical understanding of Greece before roughly 750 BCE: without writing, it is regularly asserted, we cannot build the "systematic narrative of events and circumstances relating to man in his social or civil condition," the definition that *Webster's Unabridged Dictionary* assigns to history as a craft. In addressing the larger issue of the present understanding of the

1. Stobart, *The Glory That Was Greece,* 35.

study of history, my examples derive from this cloudy realm of prehistory. And in this role, I hope that they will refute the view that the "age of heroes" belongs to the realm of myth rather than history. Not only does the evidence demonstrate actual conditions of preclassical Greece—and perhaps also events and people—but acceptance of the reality of a heroic age also allows us to view the full story of ancient Greece.

The larger theme of my lectures, and hence this book, is the current understanding of our means to gain knowledge of the past, any past. There has always been debate over the nature of history, and, in fact, opinions differ widely about whether there have been points of serious change in the basic understanding of the historical profession. Even so, from the mid-twentieth century several currents have converged to create barriers to realizing the basic purpose of all historical study, namely, the recovery and recounting of the human story. Repercussions were many and quarrelsome. One of the most serious was the depeopling of history. Only recently have lines of combat weakened to permit a calmer, less confrontational assessment of the means to understand the human past.

Much of the material of these lectures originated in earlier presentations. "Launching the Argo" began as "An Ur-Argonautica?"—a contribution to a conference titled "On Board the Argo through Time and Media." The role of archaeology in revealing the nature of preclassical Greece is explored in the book *From Citadel to City-State* and has been the subject of three recent lectures and an article for the journal *Historically Speaking*.[2] "The Birth of the Author" derives from a larger study of Hesiod and his world, currently in progress.

I am grateful to everyone who has contributed to the formulation of the material that this present account incorporates through comments on my presentations, reading of portions of the discussion, and suggestions of sources of information. Richard Johnson, fellow historian and my husband, was my companion in exploring the land of Hesiod and the reputed home of Jason. Receipt of membership in the Society of Scholars in the Simpson Center for the Humanities during the academic year 2001–2002 pro-

---

2. See Carol G. Thomas and Craig Conant, *From Citadel to City-State: The Transformation of Greece, 1200–700 B.C.E*; and Thomas, "The Greek Age of Heroes: Myth Becomes History."

vided a welcome opportunity to learn the reactions of other members to my presentation of material on which my lectures would be based. Indirectly, exposure to the presentations of others in the society provided evidence for arguments of mine from quite unexpected directions. Richard Von Kleinsmid agreed to read the entire manuscript using the trained eye of an editor; over time I have learned just how keen that eye is and greatly value his assistance. The careful editing of Annette Wenda resolved a number of issues in a final review. I am also indebted to Ethan Spanier, a doctoral student in the ancient history program at the University of Washington, who compiled the bibliography.

The business of gaining permissions is often far more difficult than shaping the text of a manuscript, but in the case of *Finding People in Early Greece* many people made the task an easy one. I thank Frances Keller and Howard Keller, yet again, for their generosity in establishing the Keller Fund in the History Department of the University of Washington to assist faculty with research and publication expenses. The fund subsidized many of the illustrations in *Finding People in Early Greece*.

Finally, I am grateful to the readers of this manuscript, whose supportive and helpful comments were delivered to me anonymously. No one of these aides, however, must be held responsible for the judgments and conclusions that I have drawn.

FINDING PEOPLE
IN EARLY GREECE

History at the Crossroads

"We historians of today," Fernand Braudel announced on December 1, 1950, "have the sense of belonging to a different age, to a different adventure of the intellect. Above all, our profession no longer seems to us to be a calm, secure undertaking." He described the situation as "History at the Crossroads." By 1958 his words were even more ominous: "There is a general crisis in the human sciences."[1]

Fear of the ramifications of the declared "crisis" did not immediately seize everyone engaged in the human sciences. Some agree with David Cannadine, director of the Institute of Historical Research at the University of London, that "[t]he notion of history in crisis seems to have been around as long as people have been writing history." According to this view, the current debate might have different points of contention than those that caused earlier controversies, but historians have long held dissimilar views of their profession. Another reason for the lack of uniform concern was that the effects of the perceived problems occurred at different rates in various fields. In a review of several books reckoning with developments in historical study, Michael Bentley speaks of "a nasty moment in the 1980s and 1990s when it looked as though epistemology might get in the way of history," whereas as early as 1968, archaeologist Jacquetta Hawkes pronounced her unhappy opinion that "there are plenty of archaeologists today who would crush this ancient city [Ninrud] and its

1. Braudel, "The Situation in History in 1950," 9; Braudel, "History and the Social Sciences: The Longue Durée," 25.

1

people under the weight of their statistics and bar all individuality from their pages."[2]

Earlier debates over the historical method were certainly serious and divisive. However, the repercussions of the crisis announced by Braudel have persisted for more than a half century and have affected not simply the discipline of history but those other disciplines whose subject is humankind as well. Some of the developments have sprung independently from the individual disciplines, yet, linked as these disciplines are by their subject, a ripple effect has spread among them, thereby deepening the cumulative consequences. New directions in other fields of study—particularly linguistics—have further complicated the assessment of the capabilities of the human-centered disciplines. In addition, historical events and scientific developments of the twentieth century that have brought momentous and worldwide changes to human life have had an equal impact on the study of that life. Thus, "History at the Crossroads" is but one part of an extensive reassessment of the efficacy of knowledge of the human past. Inasmuch as the debate engaged parties whose approaches differed greatly, the language of discussion was not always mutually comprehensible. And the outcome was of great importance—one historian drawn to "new" history admitted that "[t]here is a certain irony in our current historical understanding: it threatens to put us out of business as historians."[3] With such high stakes, debate, in writing as well as face-to-face, was often less than civil.

In sum, although tracing the nature and course of the debate is not pleasant, it is important to do so in order to appreciate the implications for the study of history. Beginning with a sketch of the factors that have been most significant in producing the reassessment, the focus will turn to their impact on the discipline of history in general and on the study of ancient history in particular. To anticipate the present state of affairs, it is encouraging to note that in the past decade signs of resolution have started to emerge.

2. Cannadine, "What Is History Today?" 5; Bentley, "Stones from the Glasshouse," 10–11; Hawkes, "The Proper Study of Mankind," 258.

3. Lynn Hunt, "President's Report," 7.

Testing the Human Sciences

By the mid-twentieth century, scholars in several fields were concerned over difficulties in their disciplines. This chapter began with the words of one of the major figures to explore the causes, the French historian Fernand Braudel. To support his perception of a general crisis in the human sciences, he explained that they are all overwhelmed by their own progress, if only because of the accumulation of new knowledge and the need to work together in a way that is yet to be properly organized. Directly or indirectly, willingly or unwillingly, none of them can remain unaffected by the progress of the more active among them.[4]

Long-established as well as more recent branches of study have been equally affected. Especially linked with the discipline of history are:

- anthropology, the study of the physical characteristics of humans as well as the nonbiological traits of human culture;

- archaeology, which is allied with anthropology and seeks to draw the most complete "picture of past human life in terms of its human and geographic environment";[5]

- sociology, the "science of those facts which taken together go to make up the collective life of man";[6]

- geography, the spatial study of society; and

- economic history, whose concern is the performance of economies through time.

A shared interest is obvious in the definitions. Less clear is why all were challenged at roughly the same time and with similar intensity.

What has been termed *midlife crisis* is apparent in several of these fields as scholars questioned the current direction of their disciplines. It is important to appreciate the relative youth of a number of the human sciences;

4. Braudel, "Longue Durée," 25.
5. Walter W. Taylor, "A Study of Archeology," 95–96.
6. Braudel, "History and Sociology," 70.

only in the late nineteenth century did archaeology, for example, progress from a search for treasures to a disciplined discovery and study of material remains from the past. Sociology, too, is rooted in the nineteenth century. As disciplines develop new evidence, rely on new tools, and thus come to new insights, evaluation of disciplinary goals and practices is to be expected. Beyond predictable reflection on procedure, however, problems arose with the growing quantity of information. At midcentury, many anthropologists and, more specifically, archaeologists began to question their use of increasingly abundant evidence and to wonder how to preserve and share it with others.

Personal experience in the early 1970s demonstrated the reality of this concern about the quantity of physical evidence. In fact, I helped to increase that quantity while participating in summer excavation in the ancient agora of Athens. The experience was made more pleasant by the invitation to stay with a young Greek woman. When we talked about the purpose of the project, her primary question was "Why is it necessary?" "We have more than enough objects from the past," she explained, "and we must pay attention to the needs of people who are living now." Simply storing the wealth of objects from the past of Greek life presents a truly serious problem in the present; construction of a road, rail line, or building is likely to uncover unexpected sites that must be examined before work on the project can continue. Construction of a subway system in Athens produced more than thirty thousand objects in the first years of the project, which is now in its eleventh year. Objects discovered must be cataloged, cleaned, and restored, then studied and published, efforts that consume countless hours and require major funding. It is fitting that some of the finds from the subway excavation are attractively displayed in the completed underground station in the center of Athens, for their intrinsic worth is considerable for the present members of the culture they represent as well as for archaeologists. Still, the ability to look at these displays does not alleviate present-day needs. Moreover, not only in Athens but also in many parts of the world, existing quantities of such objects are already so great that many items will never be displayed anywhere.

Equally serious is the question of the purpose of studying these physical remains of the past. Lewis R. Binford, who would become a major figure in reshaping archaeological method, recognized this problem in a dramatic

way after working for a year in France. His goal was to relate stone remains to other properties of archaeological sites in order to detect the kinds
of activity that combined to produce these assemblages. Binford confessed:

> I performed one correlation study after another—so many, in fact,
> that I needed a great steel trunk in order to carry all the papers back
> to the U.S. I could tell you cross-correlations between any pair of
> Mousterian tool-types, between tools and bones, between bones and
> the drip-lines in cave sites, between almost any type of data you care
> to name. What I found, of course, was many new facts that nobody
> had seen before. But none of these new facts spoke for themselves. . . .
> My metal trunk was so big and heavy that I decided to return home
> by boat and that five-day trip from Le Havre to New York gave me an
> opportunity for some disconsolate self-reflection. The whole project
> was obviously a total failure.[7]

The failure of traditional methods was perceived in other human-centered
disciplines that were not weighed down by trunks filled with bones and
tools; steadily rising numbers of records confronting sociologists, geographers, and historians were equally massive and problematic. Dealing with
the quantity of data demanded new tactics that became available at just
this time. In 1972 François Furet wrote of the "simultaneous and inter-
connected revolution and methodology and technique" that he saw in
electronic technology. Braudel put the situation plainly: "[H]uge calcula-
tions await us . . . but there are squads of calculators and of calculating
machines ready too."[8]

In addition to understanding the value of orderly sorting, many scholars in the human disciplines came to believe that study of the data was not
regularly accompanied by systematic analysis. Before 1950, the human-
centered fields had been essentially descriptive. John Habakkuk, for instance, could "think of very few economic historians before 1945 who
made any systematic use of economic theory." A growing recognition that
archaeology had not been a science gained momentum at roughly the
same time. Rather than a systematic inquiry, "it grew up with a rag-bag

7. Binford, *In Pursuit of the Past: Decoding the Archaeological Record*, 98, 100.
8. Furet, "Quantitative History," 49; Braudel, "Longue Durée," 51.

series of conventions which most archaeologists . . . have used for 'interpreting' their finds. Most such conventions have never been tested and we simply do not know whether they are valid and useful." Dissatisfaction with current aspects of the discipline combined with respect for scientific successes to produce a "new" geography in the 1950s and 1960s. "The regional tradition of descriptive synthesis and associational and loosely genetic narrative came in for particular attack."[9] Better results could be achieved, many concluded, by employing careful statistical analysis that could reveal general laws. Sociologists too began to seek answers through the methodology of the natural sciences that promotes the construction of models to assist in the formulation of general laws.

An important example of the new approach to evidence of the human past is tied to the understanding of the depth of that past. Fuller, more accurate evidence confirmed the great depth of the human story, which could no longer be measured in millennia but stretched over a million or more years. Although time has been reckoned in various ways throughout the human story, the span of the human story suggested to many that the time of the new history "cannot be measured by any of our long-established instruments." These are the words of Braudel, whose tripartite scheme has been widely adopted during the past half century. The premise underlying the scheme is that "[h]istory exists at different levels. . . . [T]he history of events works itself out in the short term: it is a sort of microhistory. Halfway down, a history of conjunctures follows a broader, slower rhythm [in cycles and intercycles]." The full extent of time—the *longue durée*—"inquires into whole centuries at a time. . . . [It] is the endless, inexhaustible history of structures and groups of structures." As Braudel states, "At first sight, the past seems to consist in [a] mass of diverse facts, some of which catch the eye, and some of which are dim and repeat themselves indefinitely. . . . But this mass does not make up all of reality." In the *longue durée,* which stretches over centuries, perhaps even millennia, "the event[s] all fit into each other neatly and without difficulty, for they are all measured on the same scale." This framework is "built . . . on

9. Habakkuk, "Economic History and Economic Theory," 29; Binford, *Pursuit of the Past,* 108; J. M. Wagstaff, "The New Archaeology and Geography," 27.

the dimensions of eternal man," not the circumstances of individual people.[10]

If an abundance of data provided the main force for a reassessment of methodology in the human-centered disciplines, a second force was, paradoxically, its limitations. Surviving evidence from the past is incomplete; we possess some bones, tools, sites, and, at times, written evidence, and in all of these categories survivals may be atypical rather than the norm. The data are also imperfect in nature: there are far more potsherds than whole pots, more fragments of human or animal bones than skeletons, more partial texts than complete accounts. Finally, the remains, especially the material evidence, are static: a picture of a settlement frozen at the moment of destruction or abandonment, the evidence of a specific funeral pyre, skeletal remains of a sole hunter accompanied by his equipment. Whereas these remains were once part of an active process, that process is not revealed by the data themselves. A more rigorous method was required to locate and explain the evidence within its own context, namely, the once interactive, interlocking system of its culture. The fragmentary pieces of the record must be set into a larger picture to become again part of the dynamic process that constitutes the subject of the human past.

Responses

How the evidence might be activated directed attention to the approaches employed in other fields that were not currently burdened by reassessment, namely, "the natural sciences, whose overwhelming success and prestige in the seventeenth and eighteenth centuries held out promise of rich fruit wherever their methods were applicable," a prestige that had expanded considerably during and after World War II. After all, the natural sciences and the human-centered disciplines had a common subject—the human story. Scientists deal with biological organisms situated in a natural environment that operates according to physical forces, the organisms that are the focus of historians, anthropologists, and sociologists, whereas geographers investigate the use of the natural environment in which these

10. Braudel, "Situation in History," 12; Braudel, "History and Sociology," 74–75; Braudel, "Longue Durée," 48, 46.

organisms dwell. By following the procedure of the natural sciences, many believed that it should be possible to find, as Isaiah Berlin puts it, "a series of natural laws connecting at one end the biological and physiological states and processes of human beings with, at the other, the equally observable patterns of their conduct—their social activities in the wider sense—and so establish a coherent system of regularities, deducible from a comparatively small number of general laws . . . a science of human behaviour."[11]

Efforts to discern the general pattern of human history are not new. Writing in the fifth century BCE, Thucydides declared that he would be satisfied if his account of the Peloponnesian War were judged useful by those who desired an exact knowledge of the past as a guide to the interpretation of the future that, in the course of human things, must resemble it (1.23). More recently, the nineteenth and early twentieth centuries received an abundance of historical "laws" from the pens of writers such as Hegel, Spengler, and Toynbee. To solve the perceived "crisis" of the mid-twentieth century, however, these conclusions were now deemed, in the words of Berlin, "too general, vague, and occasionally tautological to cast new light on anything in particular." In relying upon them, the human-related studies were, according to Braudel, disconcertingly empirical.[12] As this belief spread, the construction and testing of more specifically pointed models became fashionable in all the human disciplines. Historians sought to discern and employ general rules in order to understand individual situations; sociologists developed models to comprehend class structure and demography; economists built theoretical models and employed inferences from statistical data to interpret human economies over time. Geographers increasingly employed measurement and comparison; physical geographers particularly directed their attention to processes of change. In anthropology, perception of deeper structures underlying surface patterns became a guiding principle. For archaeologists, the construction and examination of cultural systems provided the means to introduce rigorous methodology to the study of past human life.

A common tendency links these fields: discernment of patterns that

11. Berlin, "The Concept of Scientific History," 103, 105.

12. Ibid., 118. In Braudel's words, "[S]ocial science must construct a model . . . and substitute for a disconcerting empirical reality a clearer image, and one more susceptible to scientific application" ("History and Sociology," 71–72).

emerge from the flow of seemingly isolated events. In archaeology, systems theory provided the tool to understanding significant change over time. The British archaeologist David Clarke is regularly credited with the formulation of systems analysis of cultures; Colin Renfrew quickly "activated" the approach, which is essentially a static model, to explain cultural change.[13] A system—any system—has two fundamental parameters: its environment (flora, fauna, climate, geology) and its human population. To resort to analogy, these parameters might be regarded as the anatomy of the cultural being. The anatomy of a human or animal also has individual members—arms, legs, head, internal organs—which in systems theory are known as subsystems. Five subsystems are often used in examining the nature of a culture: economic or basic subsistence, technology, social-political structure, psychological or symbolic aspects, and trade and communication. The five subsystems interact with one another and also with the environment and human population. When change occurs in one of the subsystems, the others react to absorb the change and restore equilibrium. If, however, an innovation affects all or most of the parts, a multiplier effect will bring change throughout the entire culture.

For anthropologists, a similar search for abiding properties was made possible through perception of "the deep natures or constitutions or structures or inner essences [of things] . . . normally hidden from view" from which flow the regularities that we observe. Although the definition of "structures" in geography differs from that employed by anthropologists, many geographers too adhered to "the belief that underlying the surface patterns which are readily observable and described there is a deeper reality—in the present context, socio-economic dynamics of a sort. Currents in this subterranean magma produce the surface patterns. The underlying forces are often not seen, but their configuration, it is suggested, can be inferred from surface clues."[14] Among sociologists and historians, attention shifted from individual behavior to groups of similar people—slaves, peasants, criminals, orphans—a practice akin to biological analysis of the genera and species of living things.

13. See Clarke, *Analytical Archaeology;* and Renfrew, *The Emergence of Civilisation: The Cyclades and the Aegean in the Third Millennium B.C.,* esp. chaps. 2–3, "The Explanation of Culture Change" and "The Multiplier Effect."
14. Ernest Gellner, "What Is Structuralisme?" 99; Wagstaff, "New Archaeology," 35.

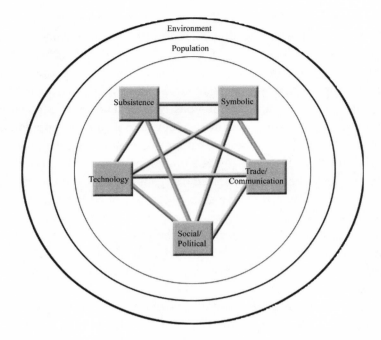

System analysis views a culture as the interplay between the human population and the natural environment that produces the basic features of a given culture: means of subsistence, technology, social-political configuration, trade and communication, and symbolic attributes. These features—called subsystems—constantly interact with one another. Innovation in one area of the existing system can affect and alter all the other areas, thus producing a new form of culture, that is, a new way of life among members of that society. (Electronically drawn by Lance Jenott)

As well as models of methodology, the natural sciences now provide the human sciences with new kinds of evidence gained from tools developed since roughly 1950. Radiocarbon dating was introduced in 1948; on its heels came trace element analysis, hydration dating, thermoluminescent dating, electronic distance meters, laser transits, isotope analysis, magnetometry, a revolution in dendrochronology (around 1965), and "a host of other absolute chronological methods; many . . . quite new . . . not yet . . . perfected," in the words of James Deetz, writing in 1967.[15]

15. Deetz, *Invitation to Archaeology,* 40. A special issue of *Archaeology* (January–February 1989) was devoted to the explosion of new tools and information and their role in the disciplines.

The field of genetics has also enhanced the study of early humans. A recent article describes the ancestry of the present population of Europe on the evidence of analysis of mitochondrial DNA (mtDNA) and finds that "the majority of extant mtDNA lineages entered Europe in several waves during the Upper Paleolithic" (that is, around 40,000–10,000 BCE). Colin Renfrew has drawn on genetic evidence to suggest another characteristic of the people who carried agriculture from Anatolia through Europe: they were, he has argued, speakers of Indo-European languages.[16]

In sum, scholars engaged in the human disciplines undertook serious reexamination of their tools and data in the mid-twentieth century. Driven by an abundance of data and an absence of rigorous methodology, they sought new tools to manage the data and new methods with which to understand them. The successful methodologies of the sciences as well as recent technological developments were seen to be answers to the dilemma. These problems and solutions stemmed from the perceived situation in the disciplines themselves; further impetus for self-examination came from developments external to scholarly research.

Factors External to the Disciplines

It is not coincidence that the "crises" in these fields came in the wake of World War II; events leading to and throughout that confrontation had an expansive reach, even beyond the horrors of the fighting between the Axis powers and the Allies. The technological and scientific developments necessary to the war effort, the international extent of involvement in the war, the terror of likely consequences should the Axis prevail, and developments of the postwar era all fueled the crisis within the human sciences.

Many of the new technologies available to scholars were consequences of needs unrelated to scholarly disciplines. World War II witnessed massive technological and scientific developments, some of which could be adapted, and were, to nonmilitary goals following the conclusion of the war. The inventor of radiocarbon dating, Willard Libby, for example, had been engaged in the study of cosmic radiation during World War II.

16. Martin Richards et al., "Tracing European Founder Lineages in the Near Eastern mtDNA Pool," quotation from the abstract, 1251. Renfrew incorporated evidence presented in Albert J. Ammerman and L. L. Cavalli-Sforza, *The Neolithic Transition and the Genetics of Populations in Europe*.

Increasingly sophisticated techniques of aerial photography and magnetic exploration below the earth's surface were tools of military intelligence before they became aids to archaeologists and geographers.

Equally significant was a less concrete consequence of the war: for millions of people, the expansion of horizons was overwhelming. Men and women who had never traveled from their homes in England, the United States, Canada, Australia, and New Zealand became part of "a globe-girdling administrative war machine" in "allied armies [that] campaigned almost as though they constituted a single trans-national force."[17]

An example may be appropriate, especially since the goal of this account is putting people back into history. In fact, developments in the twentieth century tended to remove individuals from all periods of the human story. This short sketch may help to humanize the ramifications for the millions affected by involvement in the conflict. It involves a young student of U.S. history who had just completed his master's degree when, in June 1941, he was drafted into the U.S. armed forces. Although his world had already been expanded by his having moved from a small southern town to the Boston-Cambridge area, his military service completely altered his horizons. He quickly learned that the war army was very different from the old peacetime army: the new was a mix of people from every part of the country and representing every way of life. All were compelled to adopt a uniform code of behavior. My friend gained great confidence in the ability and dedication of people who, unlike himself, had not had the advantage of a college education; many had not finished high school. He mentioned in particular the steadfast reliability of farm boys from North Dakota. After initial training, he spent nine months in Panama where, although the base was self-contained, he had regular contact with Panamanians who worked on the base. His next base was in Arizona where he trained as an aerial navigator, another stretch for one who had never been in an airplane. His lasting impression was the feeling that it was a "miracle that a plane would fly."

I like to hope that he quickly gained confidence in the flying machine, for soon he was assigned to a crew that would deliver a new plane to Australia. Because he had never flown over water before, the four-day

17. William H. McNeill, *A World History,* 443.

journey to Australia created a sense of distance that was overwhelming. Soon he experienced distancing of another kind aboard a liberty ship traveling in a convoy with ninety-nine other ships and guarded—"like herders tending sheep"—by a couple of destroyers. By sea, he could experience the separation between the United States and Italy over an entire month.

Once with the Fifteenth Air Force in Italy, his world was well defined: flying daily in a formation of five hundred planes at about twenty-three-thousand-feet altitude, he navigated his plane as it flew north to the designated target, then back to base, keeping well in mind the dire consequences of traveling too far east over Yugoslavia or northern Greece. "If we were shot down in either of those places, we should treat everyone as an enemy," he remembered. There was little opportunity to learn much of Italy or the Italians who were, of course, the enemy. He has since returned to Italy to remedy his first impression. But the lasting influence on his professional career was more encompassing: although he continued to teach and write in the field of U.S. history, his participation in the war encouraged a special interest in comparative history.

This single experience was echoed by countless lives, the total impact of which affected the study of the human past. In *What Is History?* E. H. Carr argues that historians must greatly extend their perspective beyond the traditional Western focus. Carr also urges the need to replace discussion of individual people or events with detection of larger trends and forces in the past. Theoretical frameworks are, he maintains, the tools necessary for proper detection. Once discovered, these patterns will provide a better means of understanding the present and preparing for the future.

With sales of more than a quarter million copies, the book is correctly described as "seminal-cum-perennial."[18] It draws together the concerns of "history at the crossroads," and it provided new directions at a time when higher education was rapidly expanding. At war's end, millions of former servicemen and -women began or resumed their education, aided in many cases by government subsidies. The general manager of the University of Washington Book Store, my home institution, remembers that "the summer of 1945 opened doors to a changing world for colleges and universities." Enrollment at the University of Washington was "a trickle back in

18. David Cannadine, ed., *What Is History Now?* vii.

1945 . . . became a river in 1946 and a flood in 1947."[19] Not only former service personnel but also civilians saw the merit of continuing their education beyond the primary and secondary levels. Furthermore, a population explosion was swelling numbers of potential students: in the United States alone, the 1950 population of 152 million people grew to 216 million in 1975 and 276 million in 2000, a total increase of more than 80 percent. At the same time, China's population more than doubled, whereas India's almost tripled. Existing institutions were insufficient to meet the demand, but new colleges, universities, polytechnics, and networks of community colleges arose to absorb the overflow. The audience for historical study was not only larger but also drawn from a wider spectrum of society.

Instructors too were affected by the war. A large-scale flight took scholars, especially Jewish scholars from Italy and Germany, to new homes. Large numbers of professors joined in the war effort both as servicemen and working in intelligence. Not only were their personal views of the world transformed, but the understanding of the events leading to and through the war also required more explanation than a chronicle could provide. Many of the next generation of teachers had been participants in those events. The altered view of many involved in the war effort made itself felt in the human sciences.

One consequence was the initiation of new educational programs. The postwar period saw the launching of programs in foreign-area studies developed and staffed by people who had become fluent in the languages and knowledge of cultures during the war years for military purposes. That fluency could now become a keystone to higher education. Also reflecting the appreciation of global interaction from the late 1930s and 1940s was the rise in comparative-study and interdisciplinary programs. At the same time, the rebuilding of the war-torn targets of battle brought academic disciplines into "the planning of the landscape (rural and urban) and of society itself."[20] Inasmuch as a goal of the work was to define a common cultural heritage in tangible and documentary form, historians and archaeologists were drawn into public service.

19. Lyle Goss, unpublished memoirs held in the archives of the University of Washington bookstore, 27, 32.
20. John Bintliff, "A Review of Contemporary Perspectives on the 'Meaning' of the Past," 3.

Though seemingly unrelated to the crisis felt by scholars engaged in the study of the human past, these consequences of the war years and aftermath reinforced the view that scholarship must move in different directions than it had previously followed. The two portions of the picture reinforced one another. Internally, the human-related disciplines experienced a growing accumulation of data during the first half of the twentieth century. Tools developed for military purposes associated with World War II not only produced even more data but also provided technology that could aid in assessing that evidence. A mounting concern that description of the data was insufficient turned eyes toward the method of the sciences, as well as its tools, the accomplishments of which during the war years had been so instrumental in its outcome. Inasmuch as the war involved countries located in almost every region of the globe, an understanding of previously little-known cultures was essential. Many specialists enlisted in gathering and conveying information about those once mysterious ways of life returned to peacetime occupations in higher education as members of newly established comparative and interdisciplinary programs. Consequently, the incentive to address the "crisis" in the human disciplines was powerful and widespread.

Short-Term Outcome

The impact on the study of the human past of the interlocking disciplinary and external factors associated with World War II was profound. One reaction was despair. Fernand Braudel, whose wartime experiences gave him ample good reason for personal dejection, confessed, "I myself, during a rather gloomy captivity, struggled a good deal to get away from a chronicle of those difficult years (1940–45). Rejecting events and the time in which events take place was a way of placing oneself to one side, sheltered, so as to get some sort of perspective, to be able to evaluate them better, and not wholly to believe in them."[21] He was not alone in this reaction, as we shall see in considering theoretical reactions of the second half of the century.

21. Braudel was imprisoned at Mainz from 1940 to 1942; after release, he was denounced for being a supporter of de Gaulle rather than Pétain and sent until 1945 to a discipline camp at Lübeck for enemies of Germany. See Braudel, "Longue Durée," 47; repeated in his "History and Sociology," 77.

Another result of the new approaches has been specialization due to the highly honed expertise that the new tools demanded. Sophisticated technical training is demanded of those who create computers and computer programs, develop tools for spectrographic analysis or magnetic examination of the earth, or carry out genetic examination. Expertise is equally required of people who determine the implications of these new categories of evidence. Specialization of scholarly labor is further increased by the sheer expansion of data; "subcategories" have proliferated within disciplines in which a single person might once have expected to acquire a comprehensive understanding. As a recent reviewer observed, "The days are long gone when one, or even two scholars, could master as many diverse fields as this book covers." The division of labor is especially pronounced when complex technologies are associated with the human-related disciplines.[22] An archaeologist might carry on the fieldwork, but he is likely to be accompanied by geologists, geographers, biologists, zoologists, and engineers; other specialists would be called to analyze bone finds; samples would be sent away to be tested by spectroscopic or deoxyribonucleic acid (DNA) analysis at a lab with the requisite technology and expertise. Moreover, in the wake of specialization, something of a professional trade unionism against crossing these boundaries has emerged, further separating from one another individuals engaged in the same enterprise.

An aid to manage the diverse data and findings was quickly available: computer technology could sort and analyze the mountains of information. In turn, widespread adoption of this aid produced a surge in quantitative study. Economic historians, for example, aided by computer technology, moved from the descriptive fashion prevalent before the 1950s to econometric analysis of the data, giving birth to the new economic history, cliometrics, or the measuring of Clio, the Muse of history. Sociologists have turned in the same direction, insisting "on a style of research and thinking that focuses on the testing of hypotheses based on data generated by measurements presumed to be valid." The computer first went into the field with human archaeologists in 1971, adding new capability to that study.

---

22. Mark Rose, review of *Noah's Flood*, 78. On the new technologies, see David Wilson, *The New Archaeology*, 294.

So important did quantification become that Braudel defined statistics as the universal language; statistical analysis de rigueur became a feature of most human-centered disciplines during the 1960s and early 1970s. The French scholar Emmanuel Le Roy Ladurie could announce that "[t]omorrow's historian will have to be able to programme a computer in order to survive."[23]

Quantification, respect for scientific successes, and dissatisfaction with the current descriptive character of the human-related disciplines joined forces to turn scholarship away from description to theoretical analysis. In the field of geography, descriptive synthesis gave way to careful statistical analysis that could reveal general laws. Sociologists, too, began to seek answers through the methodology of the natural sciences, which promotes the construction of models to assist in the formulation of general laws.

Not merely by employing the tools and methods of the sciences, members of the human disciplines also endeavored to join the ranks of their scientific colleagues, and, in the process, the subject of their study—humankind—was redefined. Electronic technology offered one explanation of human nature in the computational theory of mind. Mental activity consists of information, computing of information, and feedback. Memories and beliefs are products of this process, held in the structure of the brain, just as data are retained in the circuitry of a computer. Akin to the computer programs are human thinking and planning. Sense organs and motor programs link the mind to the world. More recently, progress in understanding the human genome has shaped new views of human understanding according to which "[b]ehavior is not just emitted or elicited, nor does it come directly out of culture or society. It comes from an internal struggle among mental modules with differing agendas and goals. . . . All the potential for thinking, learning, and feeling that distinguishes humans from other animals lies in the information contained in the DNA of the fertilized ovum." Put starkly by Jacquetta Hawkes, man "is nothing but a complex biochemical mechanism powered by a combustion system which energizes computers with prodigious storage facilities for retaining encoded

23. On new directions in sociology, see Orlando Patterson, "The Last Sociologist," *New York Times,* May 19, 2002, OP-ED, 19. For computer aid to archaeology, see Wilson, *The New Archaeology,* 213. Braudel, "Longue Durée," 51; Le Roy Ladurie, *The Territory of the Historian,* 6.

information."[24] In its extreme forms, these views are known as biological reductionism, a stance that identifies a human being as a living organism composed of physical, biological components. The functioning of the parts from which that organism is constructed derives from the interactive forces—chemical and molecular—of those parts.

During the second half of the twentieth century, considerable effort was invested in modeling the brain's behavior on the basis of computer network models. On analogy with digital computer programs that process information by means of operations based on strings of arbitrary symbols, mental processes consist of "a sequential series of formal rules often followed automatically." Some advocates of the similarity between computer networking and the brain believe that the tie between artificial intelligence and the mind is "more intimate than the tie between the brain and mind. . . . There is no reason to assume that higher mental functions, such as reasoning, correspond in any way to the structure of brain cells."[25]

One of the main figures in David Lodge's recent novel *Thinks* represents this perspective. "The mind is a machine, but a *virtual* machine. A system of systems," he states. Later, he continues, "The brain is more like a parallel computer [than a linear computer], in other words it's running lots of programs simultaneously." Understanding the links between these "programs"—in other words, the nature of human consciousness—is problematic, even for this director of the Centre of Cognitive Science: "[T]he problem of consciousness is basically the old mind-body one bequeathed by Descartes. . . . We know that the mind doesn't consist of some immaterial spook-stuff, the ghost in the machine. But what *does* it consist of? . . . Is it just electro-chemical activity in the brain? Neurones firing, neurotransmitters jumping across the synapses? In a sense, yes, that's all there is that we can observe."[26] In fact, a current project of the center is to design a computer that thinks and even feels in human ways.

---

24. Steven Pinker, *The Blank Slate: The Modern Denial of Human Nature,* 40, 45; Hawkes, *Nothing But or Something More,* 6.

25. Bruce Bower, "The Brain in the Machine: Biologically Inspired Computer Models Renew Debates over the Nature of Thought," 344–45.

26. Lodge, *Thinks,* 36, 38, 37.

Reactions

Multiplication of competencies and division of responsibility, especially those induced by the turn to scientific tools and methods, were not welcomed by everyone. In fact, anger has been a not uncommon reaction to the weighty influence of the sciences on the human disciplines. An outspoken critic of the "new" sociology and history speaks of the "mechanization of ideas" that quantification and theory have produced: "A mechanistic approach to history implies a mechanistic view of man."[27] Lewis Binford, who was a leader in developing new methods of interpreting archaeological data, called for a retreat from overreliance on modeling and the formulation of laws.

In a 1968 article, "The Proper Study of Mankind," Jacquetta Hawkes states her reaction in no uncertain terms: "The greatest danger in the narrow scientific outlook is the assumption that because analytical and statistical methods cannot properly be applied to values that most differentiate man from the other animals, those values must be ignored." In *Nothing But or Something More,* she vigorously addresses the view that "mentality . . . is a mere by-product of physical forces" as a "belittlement of man that goes with the breaking down of the whole person into little parts and finding nothing human in them." And she likens the new scientific tools to a technological Frankenstein's monster that must be kept in control. Equally frank is the assessment by the economic historians Douglass North and John Nye presented at the annual meeting of economic historians as recently as autumn 2002: "Four decades after the advent of the Cliometric revolution we appear to have lost our way." In the enthusiastic turn to reliance on numbers arranged in tables and graphs from which patterns could be discovered, study of the human past became a "history without people."[28] Individual people and the events in which they were involved were meaningful only as they were related to surrounding people and

27. Gertrude Himmelfarb, "Clio and the New History," 36.

28. Hawkes, "Proper Study," 259, 262; Hawkes, *Nothing But or Something More,* 29; North and Nye, cited from draft manuscript given to the author by Douglass North; Le Roy Ladurie, "History without People: The Climate as a New Province of Research," in *Territory of the Historian.*

events; by studying individuals and events in relation to others, meaningful patterns would emerge.

An important addition to the tool kit of the crisis in the human-
centered disciplines was a theoretical position grounded in absolute relativism that took root in the field of linguistics. Theories put forth by
Ferdinand de Saussure early in the twentieth century were brought to bear
on the fields of philosophy and history and then incorporated into many
of the human sciences. Moving from the realization that words often relate
to their meanings in quite arbitrary ways, Saussure proposed that words,
or signifiers, are defined by their relations to one another rather than by
relation to things they denote—the signified.[29] Language, therefore, does
not reflect reality. Subsequently, others of the same persuasion loosened
even more the connection between words and things, that is, signifiers and
signified, by arguing that every time a word is uttered, the relation with
the signified is different. Inasmuch as each individual imputes an individual meaning, no absolute, universal truths are discoverable. In sum,
by deconstructing statements into their individual components, meaning itself is deconstructed—thus the term *deconstruction,* coined by Jacques
Derrida.

It is important to realize that under the category of "texts," many advocates of deconstruction would also include material objects. Consider this
expression of the meaning to be drawn from an object surviving from the
past:

> The old pot found by an archaeologist is equivocal because it be-
> longs both to the past and to the present. . . . The pot does indeed
> preserve aspects of its time and it can be interpreted to reveal things
> about the past. So the integrity and independence of the pot does not
> mean that it does not refer outside of itself. It means that no interpre-
> tation or explanation of a pot can be attached to the pot forever,
> claiming to be integral or a necessary condition of experiencing that
> pot. . . . The autonomy of the past is also the reason why archaeolog-

29. A balanced treatment of the development, impact, and value of the theoretical position known as postmodernism is that of Richard J. Evans, *In Defence of History;* on origins, see chap. 3, pt. 4.

ical method has no monopoly on the creation of knowledges and truths about the material past. . . . People may interpret it in all sorts of different ways, according to their different interests and agendas.[30]

Such a conclusion rests on the view that individuals, both those alive now and those long departed, have characteristics and motives that are dissimilar from the characteristics and motives of others, those living now and those long dead. One consequence is that people understand the world, just as they interpret language, in different ways. The obvious conclusion is that inasmuch as it is impossible to assume the mentality of another person, it is also impossible to understand how humans in the past understood or shaped their world or any small part of it. The meaning of the old pot to its original maker, or to any of its users or to the archaeologist who has discovered it, may be quite different, or it may be the same. We simply cannot know.

Associated with the deconstructionist view of "texts" is another position based on relativism that brings together several theories under the term *postmodernism*. One element stems largely from the arguments of the French philosopher and historian Michel Foucault. Just as words are disassociated from reality, so too prevailing concepts—democracy, for instance, and ideas that all men are created equal or unequal—are produced by those people or groups most powerful at that time. Neither concepts nor ideas have an intimate connection with the "truth"; they are instead exercises in power. That is, prevailing systems of power generate conformity of thought. Established theories, it is argued, also exert pressure for conformity. Thus, texts are not products of the thoughts of individuals, but rather they arise from the current dominant discourse.

The underlying premise as put succinctly by Thomas Nagel is that "everything, including the physical world, is a social construct existing only from the perspective of this or that cognitive practice, that there is no truth but only conformity or nonconformity to the discourse of this or that community, and that the adoption of scientific theories is to be explained sociologically rather than by the probative weight of reasoning

30. Michael Shanks, *Classical Archaeology of Greece*, 124–25.

from experimental evidence." It is interesting to note that Nagel concludes, "Scientists do not believe this, but many nonscientists now do."[31]

A second element derives from a dispute within the discipline of anthropology. The long-held view that deep natures or inner essences exist within things structuring the regularities we observe was denied by the French structuralists, who argued that the essence of a symbol derived from its place in the larger system of symbols rather than from its emanation out of the underlying deep nature or structure. Again, relative position, not ties to an abiding essence, provides meaning. Individual meanings are denied in this theoretical position, named *poststructuralism.*

Yet a third component of postmodern thought originated in the United States in a challenge to the validity of the scientific approach recently adopted by the human-centered disciplines as well as in criticism of the values and institutions of the current society and its culture. The arts and architecture became visual expressions of the challenge in the appearance of pop art and eclectic architectural styles, while political activism was a verbal expression of the critique. Drawing on theories embodied in deconstruction and poststructuralism, postmodernism has become an umbrella definition, particularly among American intellectuals.[32]

It was not long before the theory spread from France into other parts of Europe and then to the United States; it also quickly moved from linguistics to other disciplines. Although it found converts, it also caused angry debate. A letter in the 1970s from a colleague at Cambridge University described a heated meeting of the faculty over the wisdom of allowing deconstructionism into the Cambridge curriculum in any form. And in *My Strange Quest for Mensonge,* a brilliant satire of the movement, Malcolm Bradbury recounts how

> the entire English faculty suddenly erupted in uproar and internecine strife over this extraordinary new matter. The issue, fanned by the popular press and an opportunist Labour party, even came to

31. "The Sleep of Reason," review of *Fashionable Nonsense: Postmodern Intellectuals' Abuse of Science,* by Alan Sokal and Jean Bricmont, *New Republic,* October 12, 1998, 32–38; quotations on p. 36.

32. For a useful discussion of this development, see David S. Whitley, "New Approaches to Old Problems: Archaeology in Search of an Ever Elusive Past."

threaten the government, and risk the stability of the pound sterling.
. . . [B]y the middle of the 1970s, the Structuralist and thereafter the
Deconstructionist affair was . . . creating that worldwide upheaval in
thinking that has made it inescapable for anyone who cares to have a
thought about anything.

Its spread, as Bradbury graphically describes,

required a whole new look at the entire tradition of thought and
writing, and the great unmasking of the errors of the past by the mis-
readings of the present proceeded apace. Not only did the new theory prove that the cupboard of Western thought was now bare; it
showed it had always been *completely empty in the first place.* Now
was the time to demystify and denude, revealing to the world that
not only the emperor but every single one of his subjects was either
not wearing clothes at all, or did so only because they had been role-
and gender-typed.

Bradbury continues, "[I]f we are to make sense of Deconstruction at all,
and goodness knows it is a difficult enough task even on a very good day,"
we must realize that "the whole affair is nothing other than a profound
modern philosophy *of,* precisely, absences." This does make for problems:

[I]f the author was dead, it was still necessary to have a Deconstructionist author who could explain this to us. Though the book
was dead, someone or something had to explain this in the Deconstructionist book. The subject might be proven subjectless, but it was
necessary for somebody, or some body, to prove this to us. Thus
Deconstruction had to establish an authority that was beyond authority, an interpretation that was beyond interpretation, a presence
that was beyond absence, a non-transcendental transcendental beyond the grave.[33]

Bradbury's book is good fun, but the quarrels provoked by the new theories were not at all laughable.

33. Bradbury, *My Strange Quest,* 13, 16, 20, 21, 24.

Outcome in the 1980s and 1990s

Efforts to solve the perceived crisis in the human sciences were sufficient to produce "new" disciplines in all of the human sciences: new economic history, also known as econometrics or cliometrics; new sociology; new anthropology; new archaeology; new geography; and new history. Because the fields were responding to similar stimuli, characteristics of the "newness" were remarkably similar.

So strong was the influence of the methods of the natural sciences that every discipline has adopted a hypothetico-deductive approach, new tools, and statistical analysis. That analysis has moved from simple statistical work into mathematical modeling. At the same time, the emergence of specialized methodologies resulted in a proliferation of new areas within traditional fields. The combination of complex methodologies and division into highly specialized areas of expertise brought an implosion of new information but, at the same time, increased the difficulties of communication within and between fields. One notable result of these developments has been a decline of interest in human activity. In geography, for example, "the interplay of physical conditions and human activity became perhaps more of an intellectual embarrassment than a challenge."[34]

Although the new approaches were widely adopted, the developments have also bred a countercurrent in the 1980s and 1990s. The word *crisis* has again been in vogue, as many worry that the new approaches show a serious lack of context for the models, rely overmuch on statistical analysis, attempt to quantify the unquantifiable, speak in language that only specialists can understand, and make dubious assumptions about human behavior and motivation, if humans are allowed any part in the picture.[35]

The developments affected all of the related disciplines, albeit at different times and with varying degrees of impact of the new methods. While keeping the larger context in mind, let us turn to the situation for historical studies that, during the past forty years, became for many the "new history." In the creation of the "new" discipline, methods, objectives, the

34. Wagstaff, "New Archaeology," 29.
35. Pat Hudson, *Encyclopedia of Historians and Historical Writing*, 348. Although this list of concerns is directed to economic history, it applies to all other related fields.

contents of professional writing, conferences, and curricula in primary and secondary education have been transformed in major ways.

Publication of G. M. Trevelyan's *English Social History* in 1944 has often served to mark a turning away from traditional historical scholarship. The author's own description of his study indicates the reason it defines what would soon be termed the *new history:* it is "the history of a people with politics left out," a study intended to discuss ordinary men and women, thereby correcting the imbalance that resulted from concentration on major events, great leaders, and important intellectuals. Seminal social histories had appeared earlier in the century, but the shift in the balance beam inclined more and more in the 1950s and 1960s.

It was encouraged by the availability of computer technology that had become less expensive during the 1960s. Eagerly adopted to deal with growing quantities of data, computers enabled quantitative history of large aggregate groups. As we have seen, the expanded worldview resulting from events of World War II made plain the importance of understanding cultural groups, not merely important figures in the history of various states. Given the focus on ordinary, often anonymous people, it is not surprising that methods employed in other social science disciplines were increasingly utilized: sociology, anthropology, economics, and Freudian psychology were especially valuable, as they were concerned with "every-person," or the "eternal" human, not just "elite" figures.

The term *social history* describes this focus on "every-person." It consists of several main branches: social problems, everyday life, common folk, and, more recently, women's history. Even those who find it dangerous recognize its importance. It retains the subject of history—people—although through study of anonymous categories that have previously been largely ignored. Postmodernism, by contrast, essentially removes the human element; in its denial of meaning in evidence from the past, postmodernist theory is "antithetical to both history and truth"; in fact, it "involves a repudiation of the historical enterprise as it has been understood and practiced until very recently."[36] On the grounds that textual evidence is understood in a particular way by each individual author or reader,

36. Gertrude Himmelfarb, "Postmodernist History," 71.

there can be no absolute truth. An "event" in the past is simply a "text" in the present, a text that will be variously "read." Each and every would-be historian, as a consequence, creates his or her own account, even when all rely on the same "texts."

To be sure, disagreement over the proper study of history is not new. In the dawn of the appearance of the discipline, Thucydides, treading in the footsteps of Herodotus, "father of history," openly declared his departure from his predecessor in writing a work "not as an essay to win the applause of the moment, but as a possession for all times" (1.23). Why has the reaction to new approaches been so abrasive?

The emergence of new fields within history contributed to the situation. The specialization that accompanied adoption of highly technical tools by the human-related disciplines carried into the subfields within the disciplines themselves. Depending upon one's approach to history, a person came to be defined as a social, psychological, demographic, diplomatic, political, or cultural historian. Growing quantities of evidence produced another division within those categories, as scholars were trained as ancient, medieval, modern, or postmodern historians. A third division followed in the realization that global understanding of the past was essential to the present, and thus, one taught, wrote, and read the history of China, India, Russia, Latin America, Britain, France, Germany, Italy, southeast Asia, Africa, or Canada, and regularly only a temporal and special portion of those main dividers. If one studies antiquity, fifth-century Athens can more than fill a lifetime of investigation. As Lawrence Stone describes the outburst, "This list could be extended indefinitely. . . . [T]he output represents the most stunning explosion of the historical discipline since it first began in the early nineteenth century."[37]

A consequence of the specialization was a rising inability among people even within the same discipline to communicate with one another. The American Historical Association (AHA) currently has 115 affiliates; many of those organizations plan sessions at the annual meeting of the AHA in early January. Those sessions do draw an audience, generally one of colleagues in that particular subject. Moreover, a good number of those affil-

---

37. Stone, "Resisting the New," review of *The New History and the Old*, by Gertrude Himmelfarb, *New York Review*, December 17, 1987, 59.

iates are independent societies that organize their own annual meetings and publish journals in their members' area of interest. When time and funds demand a choice of which annual meeting to attend, scholars often opt for that of their independent society, especially if their field of teaching and research is not affiliated with the AHA, as is the case, for example, of the Organization of American Historians.

Another explanation for the decline in communication rests in the strident positions taken by both advocates of the "new" history and those wedded, at least partly, to more traditional approaches. For some scholars persuaded of the merits of social history, for example, this approach is more than one additional way of studying the past; it should be THE approach to history. Gertrude Himmelfarb asserts, "[M]y objections are not to social history as such but to its claims of dominance, superiority, even 'totality'—not to social history as it may complement or supplement traditional history but to that which would supplant it." If history adopts the sociological mode, Himmelfarb believes, it can become an account of anonymous masses, groups of people devoid of ideas, beliefs, principles, and perceptions. The writer of a review in the *Economist* understood that same danger: that "concern for minutiae of social history in the laudable pursuit of past mentalités can trivialize study of the past." The appearance of a study of toilet training in Merovingian Gaul would be a "signal for worry." Or, as Paul Johnson concludes in similar vein, "[A]s with other sensible ideas, this [focus on ordinary men and women] has been carried beyond reason by fanatics and doctrinaires, especially by those academics who got tenure during the big university expansions in the 1960s."[38]

The relativism of postmodernist thought nearly annihilated meaningful conversation about the past in the present. On the one hand, every person—whether alive today or dead long ago—relates to and understands his or her world individually. We cannot step inside the mind of another in attempting to "read" the "text" (that is, the evidence) provided to us. The presumed actors in the past are individuals whose intentions, motivations,

---

38. Himmelfarb, "History with the Politics Left Out," 26; Himmelfarb, "Two Nations or Five Classes," 69; "Redressing the Balance," review of *The New History and the Old*, by Himmelfarb, *Economist* (November 14, 1987): 106–8; Johnson, "Why Big Politics Always Counts," review of *The New History and the Old*, by Himmelfarb, *Los Angeles Times Book Reviews*, September 27, 1987, 1.

and values cannot be recovered. Thus, as postmodernists, we must agree with Michel Foucault's sad conclusion: "To all those who still wish to talk about man, about his reign of his liberation, to all those who still ask themselves questions about what man is in his essence, to all those who wish to take him as their starting-point in their attempts to reach the truth, to all these warped and twisted forms of reflection we can answer only with a philosophical laugh—which means, to a certain extent, a silent one." We must understand, if persuaded by postmodern relativism, that discussion in the present can produce no greater truth. Himmelfarb recounts a discussion at a symposium on new trends in history at which one speaker admitted that "there was no meeting ground between [two people studying the same subject] and there need not be."[39]

The rift has assumed concrete form in the creation of a new historical society—"new" as in "alternative," rather than "new" in the sense of designating the "new" history. Its intent is to provide a forum for nonnew practitioners of the art of history in an atmosphere that one of its primary founders and its first president, Eugene D. Genovese, described as "uncomfortably resembl[ing] the McCarthyism of the 1950s." Founded in 1998, its goal is "to rescue history from the overspecialization, trivialization, faddishness, and political exclusivity into which the main historical organizations and no small number of departments have fallen." Consequently, he continued, "We have founded The Historical Society to foster the intellectual and ideological openness that alone nurture rich and challenging historical work of every variety. All we ask of our members [is] that they lay down plausible premises; reason logically; appeal to evidence; and respect the integrity of all those who do the same." In the same year, Marc Trachtenberg wrote "The Past under Siege" and admitted that he was "astonished by the response" reflected in the rise in membership in the new society.[40]

As of August 2004, the Historical Society has approximately fifteen

39. Foucault, *The Order of Things: An Archaeology of the Human Sciences,* 342–43; Himmelfarb, "Two Nations or Five Classes," 47.

40. Genovese, "A New Departure," in *Reconstructing History: The Emergence of a New Historical Society,* ed. E. Fox-Genovese and E. Lasch-Quinn, 7–9; Trachtenberg, "The Past under Siege," 9–11. Originally published as "Restoring Dignity to the Historical Profession," *Wall Street Journal,* July 17, 1998.

hundred members.[41] It has generated regional societies throughout the United States and a branch located in Paris. It publishes the *Journal of the Historical Society* and a bulletin, *Historically Speaking,* and organizes a national conference that avoids panels "whose participants 'construct' and 'deconstruct' and speak of 'representation,' 'discourse,' 'gender,' and 'bodies' in tortured phrases seemingly mistranslated from the original Bulgarian." Its conference in 2000 focused on the study of revolutions; however, "no one called for an armed uprising, and blessedly, there was no mention of bodies."[42]

Such wrangling may have a bearing on professional scholars, but does it have any bearing on the lives of others? The current problems in the U.S. educational system indicate that it does. Continuing slippage in younger students' knowledge of history was cause for sufficient serious concern by the 1980s to give rise to a project intended to correct the situation. Research and study produced the drafting of national standards in basic curricular areas: mathematics, science, English, the arts, foreign languages, geography, and civics, as well as history. Funding to develop the history standards was awarded by both the U.S. Department of Education and the National Endowment for the Humanities (NEH). Just days prior to the publication of the national history standards, the then chairperson of the NEH challenged the adequacy of the proposed standards as "a paradigm of political correctness that emphasized race and gender while ignoring traditional heroes, and that magnified the failings of American society while belittling its accomplishments."[43]

A revision followed that, at best, mollified the antagonism but did not provide much satisfaction. As one of the participants in the process has written, "The story does not end happily. . . . We seem to be back where we started, having taken a circuitous route that involved lots of bruises, injuries, and split lips." Perhaps, she concludes, there is no middle ground between the two camps. The conclusion is sad in light of the current understanding of the past by those who have passed through our secondary

41. E-mail message from Donald Yerxa, editor of the society's *Historically Speaking,* summer 2004.

42. George Huppert, "President's Corner."

43. Quoted by Diane Ravitch, "The Controversy of National History Standards," in *Reconstructing History,* ed. Fox-Genovese and Lasch-Quinn, 244.

schools. As recently as 1995, "57 percent of high school seniors scored 'below basic' in their knowledge of American history." Walter McDougall, professor of history at the University of Pennsylvania, conveys the sadness more vividly: "Those kids are bleeding. I see it every semester in my Ivy League classrooms. Graduate students who are ignorant of the bare skeleton of the historical narrative. Honor students who cannot write grammatical English. Average students who cannot write, do not read, and will not think. Or are intimidated."[44]

Is Ancient History Immune?

These developments and attitudes characterize the conception of historical study in general, and the study of ancient history has not escaped their effect. The "crisis" in ancient history was perceived early in the 1950s. Arnaldo Momigliano stated in his 1952 inaugural lecture in London that "all students of ancient history know in their heart that Greek history is passing through a crisis."[45] If anything, the impact has been particularly severe because the study of antiquity is so reliant on other disciplines that have been caught up in the theories and approaches that have created the "new" history. Above all, the disciplines of archaeology and philology are essential to an understanding of the ancient world. There is now a "new" archaeology, and new criticism has become popular among classical philologists.

Archaeology

In setting the stage for the perceived "crisis" in the human-related disciplines, I noted the role played by the growing bulk of physical evidence, keenly felt by archaeologists. Lewis Binford, described as "the man who put it all together and made archeological theory exciting in the 1960s," admitted, "Archaeology in the 1960s is at a major point of evolutionary change." In 1974, David Wilson included chapters in his account *The New*

44. Ibid., 248, 249; 1995 statistics quoted in "An Educational Mission: Standards for the Teaching of History," pt. 4 in ibid., 237; McDougall, "Whose History? Whose Standards?" in ibid., 297.

45. Reprinted in G. W. Bowersock and T. J. Cornell, eds., *Studies on Modern Scholarship*. Not only was Momigliano convinced of the situation by his knowledge of the current study of ancient history, but he was also affected by World War II as a refugee from Fascist Italy.

A response to the "new" archaeology in the form of a cartoon drawn by Pierre Laurent on the inside cover of an offprint by D. de Sonneville-Bordes (1966). (Published in Lewis R. Binford, In Pursuit of the Past *[New York: Thames and Hudson, 1983])*

Archaeology titled "Crisis in the Profession" and "Crisis in Theory," recounting the "several waves of pessimism in the late 1950s and 1960s." And because "[a]rchaeology, by etymology the study of beginnings, has historical reconstruction for its objective," the throes of the discipline of archaeology have been keenly felt in historical study, especially in those periods for which physical evidence is a major source of information.[46]

Archaeology was a leader in adopting new scientific technologies since, of the human-centered disciplines, archaeology is one of the most reliant on scientific tools to locate, catalog, and analyze evidence. The current tool kit of archaeologists includes magnetometers, trace element analysis, electronic distance meters, lasers, robots, tools for underwater excavation, devices for echo sounding, tools for aerial reconnaissance, the means of analyzing deoxyribonucleic acid extracted from bones and teeth of ancient human remains, and, of course, computers. Dates are learned through techniques that use radiocarbon, hydration, dendrochronology, geochronology, potassium-argon, uranium, fission tracking, obsidian hydration, amino-acid racemization, analysis of charged atoms, electron spin resonance, archaeomagnetism, and thermoluminescence. The quantity of data has grown exponentially as a result of these techniques.

Suddenly, archaeologists were presented with not only more data but also data of another order. What was lacking was "a testing program aimed at evaluating the utility and accuracy of ideas. This procedure was science. The scientific method was never a component of traditional archaeology; only the fit between generalization and the data was commonly evaluated under the older procedures."[47] I have noted the popularity of systems analysis, a tool that archaeologists regularly employed. Another solution that has had wide appeal is middle-range theory, initially formulated by Lewis Binford, which seeks the development of a distinct body of theory that can bridge the gap between the data and generalized propositions. By positing the way in which the archaeological record reflects behavior in the past, it stands between the body of data and the largest questions asked

46. Richard A. Watson, "The 'New Archeology' of the 1960s," 212; Binford, "Archeological Perspectives," in *New Perspectives in Archaeology,* ed. Sally R. Binford and Lewis R. Binford, 27; Wilson, *The New Archaeology,* 192; *Encyclopedia of the Social Sciences,* s.v. "Archaeology."

47. Binford, "The 'New Archaeology,' Then and Now," 56.

of it. For instance, it is unlikely, a middle-range thesis might state, that potsherds can reflect individual perceptions of the world.

The proliferation of tools, theoretical approaches, and quantification has brought the same explosion of subfields that have blossomed in the related fields studying the human past. Some of the newer camps are structural, cognitive, Marxist, processual and postprocessual, experimental, critical, and survey archaeology and, surviving from the earlier days of the discipline, traditional excavation, although in virtually every project scientific tools have altered the nature of excavating. Realization of the changes in the disciplines is quickly demonstrated by the titles of Binford's own publications: his Ph.D. dissertation, completed in 1964, was descriptively titled "Archaeological and Ethnohistoric Investigations of Cultural Diversity and Progressive Development among Aboriginal Cultures of Coastal Virginia and North Carolina," whereas 2001 saw the appearance of *Constructing Frames of Reference: An Analytical Method for Archaeological Theory Building Using Hunter-Gatherer and Environmental Data Sets.*

Moreover, archaeology felt the impact of the critical theory that informs deconstructionism and postmodernism. Some view objects, we have seen, as "texts" that must be read. Although these objects are remnants of the past, their meaning is buried with the past, on the view that it is impossible for a person of a different age to directly experience the past. Thus, "it is impossible to truly know the past." Furthermore, each person confronting the past does so through his or her own distinct perspective, values, and goals. Consequently, the reconstruction of that evidence will reflect these differences; no common interpretation can emerge. A solution to this state of affairs put forth by Ilya Berelov is that "archaeology in its activity should return to its innocent state and in this way become a self-conscious propagator of myth."[48]

Exponents of particular archaeological perspectives are no more civil to one another than are new and traditional historians in their debates. In the second edition of their *Re-constructing Archaeology,* Michael Shanks and Christopher Tilley admit, "We chose to be confrontational, polemical,

---

48. Michael Shanks and Christopher Tilley, *Re-constructing Archaeology: Theory and Practice,* 11–12; Berelov, "Metamythics: The Epistemological Problems of Archaeology," 103, following I. Bapty, "Nietzsche, Derrida, Foucault: ReExcavating the Meaning of Archaeology," 274.

anti-dogmatic and critical, and not simply as a rhetorical gesture. We were ready to push supposed liberal academic debate to its limits." They have been answered in like manner.[49] In sum, the appearance of disputatious quarreling over proper theory has tended, in some circles, to replace discussion of the evidence itself. Even Binford now reminds adherents of the new archaeology that theories and models cannot replace discussion of the evidence.

Philology

Written evidence joins material remains even for preclassical Greek history, albeit in a limited way, in the Linear B records for the Mycenaean age, the Homeric epics and other works joined to the Homeric cycle, Hesiod's poems, and a few inscriptions from the late Dark Age. From the seventh century on, surviving written records increase in quantity and diversity. Study of these sources constitutes the work of classicists and departments of classics, often claimed to be the oldest field in higher education. There is no debate on the view that historians of antiquity must command a thorough understanding of the written sources. However, a contingent of classical scholars has been persuaded by the proclaimed merits of new ways of employing and understanding these sources. Publications of the past twenty years show the rise of interest in (1) applying statistical tools; (2) deconstructing the units of text; (3) reading texts through particular eyes—say, of a woman or a victim of established power—and, more generally, denying the fixity of any single reading; and (4) applying theoretical models to the texts.

These brief descriptions reveal the impact of responses to the perceived crisis in the human-related disciplines that we have been tracking from the mid-twentieth century: use of scientific tools, particularly the computer, to conduct quantificational analysis of the evidence; adaptation of the linguistic theory of deconstruction to classical texts; the force of postmodern objection to the reading of texts through a single vision, especially one deriving from prevailing systems of power; and the value placed on theoretical models. It is true that the new directions enlivened the study of

49. Shanks and Tilley, *Re-constructing Archaeology,* xix. On them being answered, the articles in *Norwegian Archaeological Review* 22 (1989) confront these perspectives.

classics, producing new fields of study, journals, and societies. But, as in many instances of innovation, the results were such a departure from the long-established tradition that they provoked a strong, negative reaction.[50]

Quoting the words of five converts to the "new" classics will suggest the outcome of the new centers of attention.

Statistical Tools

A total of 101 different PNV forms (counting elided and non-elided PNVs separately) are used in all 551 times to address 89 different characters in the *Iliad* and *Odyssey*. Of the total attestations, 281 occurrences of 69 PNV forms (. . . 50.10 percent), belonging to 63 characters, are verse initial.[51]

Deconstruction of Units

The knot of crossing contradictions becomes insoluble: the subjectivity of the hero emerges with the auto-affection that is exercised by a discourse/voice which is "other" (*kleos*); glory (*kleos*) is the effect of a repeated voice that insistently declares this effect to be a valuable (divine) voice and a valueless rumour; *eukhos* is either a variant of that same voice, or "victory," which is meaningless since it is a momentary result of the gamble. . . .

The power of the negative that I have liberated with this reading deeply shakes all the articulations that should hold the text tightly together. We are left, to some extent, in a predicament or *aporia* that would seem to force the reader into silence.[52]

---

50. In my lectures at the University of Missouri in September 2002, I took an adamant stance regarding this direction in classical studies. I am grateful to Daniel Hooley, professor and current chair of the Classics Department at that university, for a fruitful conversation that has caused me to appreciate the positive aspects of the new approaches. As a firm believer in the view that a prevailing thesis is likely to produce an antithesis that, in turn, will produce a new and different thesis, I am hopeful that the once-new will not eliminate, but rather enliven, the earlier approach to the study of classical literature.

51. Ahuvia Kahane, *The Interpretation of Order: A Study in the Poetics of Homeric Repetition*, 83.

52. P. Pucci, "Banter and Banquets for Heroic Death," 150.

Reading through Particular Eyes

The strength of Odysseus' desire to return can be explained then as desire to arrive where he can found Western civilization on the myth of the consent of the oppressed.[53]

Denying the Fixity of Any Single Reading

Against the horizon of the already and of overtaking, temporarity finds itself disclosed in the concealing-revealing of tragedy. The disclosure does not merely show the nature of this temporarity, but shows its transition into a new already passing into the future, hence our feeling that concealing revealing, instead of being polarized at one or another "end" of the temporal spectrum, hovers on a threshold. There overtaking suddenly reveals the presently futural as the already and just as suddenly vanishes into concealment.[54]

Applying Models and Formulas

In an examination of thirteen passages in the *Iliad*, K. Scott Morell considers characters pulled in various directions who pause in order to decide what to do. He considers

> the characters' focalization (NF_2), when they cannot explain or predict certain outcomes because of the "butterfly effect," the nonlinear nature of dynamic systems characterized by extreme sensitivity to initial conditions . . . moments of inner deliberation appear in complex narrator-text, passages narrative by the external narrator-focalizer (NF_1), but focalized through a character or characters (F_x). Deities do not intervene when the narrative describes the inner deliberation through character-text ($NF_2 = C_x (\rightarrow) NeFe_2 = C_x$. This illustrates the inclination of the tradition to locate the activities of the deities primarily in the focalization of the external narrator.[55]

53. Elizabeth Gregory, "Unraveling Penelope: The Construction of the Faithful Wife in Homer's Heroines," 18.

54. D. Halliburton, "Concealing Revealing: A Perspective on Greek Tragedy," 265.

55. Morrell, "Chaos Theory and the Oral Tradition: Nonlinearity and Bifurcation in the *Iliad*," 121.

Such studies did produce dismay. In their book *Who Killed Homer?*—to date the most detailed and outspoken attack on recent developments—Victor Davis Hanson and John Heath offer perhaps the truest comment on responding to efforts of these kinds: "Sometimes all a reader can do is sit back and watch the words go by." But there is anger as well. Reviewing a study of Propertius, J. L. Butrica summarizes its author's effort as trying "to persuade his readers that 'conventional scholarship' has failed and must fail with Propertius because it seeks to apply to him the aesthetic values of his own age rather than those of ours." Butrica concludes in saddened wonderment "that a book such as this one would ever have been conceived much less published."[56]

Hanson and Heath's claim that although careerism and elitist attitudes have burgeoned among the current generation of classical scholars, "the self-proclaimed Old Guard of Classics fiddled while Rome and Greece burned in their classrooms." They assert, "The authors of this [new] stuff often do not believe it themselves! So brazen are some Classicists, in fact, that they apparently publish their own hypocrisy." As in the fields of history and archaeology, civility is hard to find. In his review of the book, Thomas Palaima speaks of the "internecine warfare" of the sort that *Who Killed Homer?* tries to foment. Frank Frost describes the book's tone as "take no prisoners mode," whereas J. Bottum's review in the *Wall Street Journal* titled "It's War!" proposes: "With a recent battle among classicists, the academic world has reached a martial intensity unseen since Rome destroyed Carthage and sowed salt over the ruins." Combat extends to the personal level. In a reply to two reviews of their book, Hanson and Heath ask of one reviewer, "What 1980s tar pit did this postmodern stegosaurus lumber out from?" and say of another, "[His] machine gun spray left a fascinating pattern on the wall. But we're still not sure what he was aiming at. Still, at least he is funny and can write, and his passive-aggressive drive-by proves—if anyone had any doubts—that he is by now well beyond good and evil."[57] With such hostility, can there be dialogue among people in the present whose proclaimed interest is human experience in the past?

56. Hanson and Heath, *Who Killed Homer? The Demise of Classical Education and the Recovery of Greek Wisdom*, 138; Butrica, review of *Propertius: Modernist Poet of Antiquity*, 268.

57. Hanson and Heath, *Who Killed Homer?* 85, 142; Palaima, "Classics: Apocalypse Now or Working toward the Future?"; Frost, review of *Who Killed Homer?* by Hanson and

Effect on the Study of Ancient History

Perhaps the most significant consequence of these diverse developments of the past half century is that the human-related disciplines have lost sight of their subject. A spillover effect intensified the impact of both the crisis and the reaction to it. In the bargain, many of those engaged in those sciences have lost something of their own humanity. Brief reiteration of the perceived difficulty shows how people have been omitted from a prominent position in the process.

First, the surfeit of data encouraged scholars to seek new means and tools to understand the evidence. Before roughly the middle of the past century, the common approach of these disciplines was descriptive, with attention trained on specific people, objects, or events. The search for a more sophisticated means of understanding and reporting the data drew scholars to the approach of the natural sciences. Laws might be discovered, many believed, that would move beyond the mass of particulars to universal principles. To determine these laws required model- and theory-building and testing. Happily, new tools were at hand to manage the existing data. The computer was welcome in organizing and sorting the evidence into categories that could be compared with one another. Cohorts of quantifiers and statisticians joined the ranks of historians, geographers, economists, sociologists, anthropologists, and archaeologists.

The new tools and methods produced new insights that, in turn, expanded the data even more. One insight was the depth of the human past, which seems to be constantly receding. Scientific tools were available to calculate this depth, which now reached well beyond the point for which any record of individuals existed. Rather, one now dealt with "eternal" humankind. The *longue durée,* as we have seen, is "the endless, inexhaustible history of structures and groups of structures."[58] The story of the human past also exploded in breadth, aided by the growing interconnections among once quite separated cultures. Encouraged by the popularity of quantification, scholars took refuge in the study of broad cultural traditions produced by anonymous humankind.

Heath; Bottum, "It's War!" *Wall Street Journal,* May 28, 1999, Weekend Taste sec., W11; response of the authors in *Bryn Mawr Classical Review,* 98.5.14.

58. Braudel, "History and Sociology," 74–75.

The anonymity of our human ancestors was only intensified by the emergence of postmodernist thought. The collective impact of the "new humanities," as Keith Windschuttle has summarized it, is the undermining of the methodology of historical research, destruction of the distinction between history and fiction, and creation of the impossibility to access the past in the contention "that we have no proper grounds for believing that a past independent of ourselves ever took place."[59]

Many have followed the advice of Albert Demangeon, "Let us give up considering men as individuals." In fact, adherence to the relativism of postmodernist belief does away with both the object and the analyst of the human past. Responses to this situation vary from confusion to a kind of sadness or outspoken anger and even a call to return to previous approaches to our subject. In describing what he calls "the present confusion," Colin Renfrew cautions, "There is, indeed, a risk that archaeologists are beginning to think in terms of 'isms,' of supposedly new frameworks of thought, each superseding the defects of the recent but ultimately unfashionable framework or ism, now to be rejected." For Stuart Manning, "There are no people, just broad patterns and processes." In some estimations, the outcome has been even more serious: as Richard J. Evans states starkly, in the 1990s some "began to question not only the possibility of reaching any objective interpretation or understanding of the past, but even the possibility of knowing anything for certain about the past at all." Clifford Geertz has asked, "The question is, of course, how anyone who believes all this can write anything at all, much less go so far as to publish it."[60]

Attempts to remedy the perceived confusion are apparent in all the disciplines affected by the immediate response to the concerns of the post–World War II years. Reactions against the dehumanization that had occurred call for repeopling the study of the past. Exciting scholarship in economic history during the past decade or so is based on new appreciation of individual actors. By contrast with neoclassical economic theory

59. Windschuttle, *The Killing of History*, 36.
60. Demangeon, *Problèmes*, as quoted in Braudel, "Is There a Geography of Biological Man?" 115; Renfrew, "Explanation Revisited," 8; Manning, "From Process to People: Longue Durée to History," 315; Evans, *In Defence of History*, 7; Geertz, *Works and Lives: The Anthropologist as Author*, 96.

that "modeled a frictionless and static world," leaders in recent study of economic change, like Douglass North, believe that "[e]conomic change is a ubiquitous, ongoing, incremental process that is a consequence of the choices individual actors and entrepreneurs of organizations are making every day." And to understand the human role, it is necessary to comprehend the workings of the mind and its interplay with the societal "stock of knowledge," a path leading directly to other natural and social sciences. Although the constraints are considerable, individual response occurs on every level: minds are genetically different, interactions with the physical environment can vary from person to person, influence from the sociocultural environment also differs, and participation in, or acceptance of, societal beliefs is not uniform among all members of a society. As North states, "Self conscious modeling of this interaction at a moment of time, much

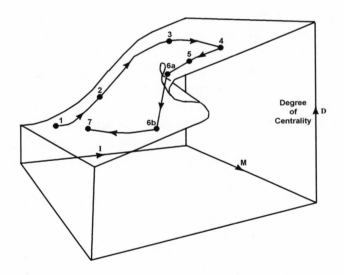

Model of system collapse. Cusp catastrophe is a model of the collapse of a system, that is, culture. When forces reach a point of tension, the existing situation suddenly reverses in the opposite direction. From states 1 through 4, investment in charismatic authority (I) promotes a greater degree of central control (D), resulting in a weakening of the power, or growing marginality, of the rural population (M). Point 6 marks the cusp or reversal of those trends. (Electronically drawn by Lance Jenott)

less over time, has not been part of the agenda of economists, development economists, or economic historians."[61] From the perspective of our interest in the human role in history, this is not the "dismal science" that economics has been styled.

Reactions against biological reductionism and the computational theory of mind began in the wake of advocacy of them. It is interesting that David Lodge's second protagonist in his novel *Thinks* is a literary scholar who finds abhorrent the view that "each of us is . . . a parallel processing computer running by itself without an operator." Rather, she knows that "human consciousness is uniquely capable of imagining that which is not physically present to the senses, capable of imagining things which do not exist, capable of creating imaginary worlds . . . and capable of abstract thought." The fictional debate is paralleled among scientists. Steven Pinker, for example, though stressing the importance of genetic composition, acknowledges that it is wrong to attribute every element of cognition to the genes. The first reason for the inaccuracy of this attribution is that "most effects of genes are probabilistic," whereas "[t]he second reason that genes aren't everything is that their effects can vary depending on the environment." Even greater stress on the environment makes it an equal partner in producing and enlarging cognitive powers of the brain. In his book *A Mind So Rare*, Merlin Donald describes the neurobiological nature of the brain but shows convincingly that human consciousness amounts to much more than the sum of its neuroanatomical parts. The brain must possess the innate capacity to find, filter, and remember the essential features of that environment. "Modern human awareness is shot through with cultural influences, and regardless of its physical boundaries, it is in the firm grip of the cultural web. Connected minds prosper in proportion to the richness of their links with culture. The creative collision between the conscious mind and distributed cultural systems has altered the very form of human cognition." Thus, the equation of the brain with the network of a computer has not persuaded everyone. Donald's argument even has space for individual impact on the cultural context: "Under the right circumstances, the cognitive resources of an entire culture can become

61. North, "Economic Performance through Time"; North, draft of "Institutions and the Performance of Economies over Time," 7.

concentrated inside a single mind, and this can bring about an awesome concatenation of forces."[62]

The awareness of an ever deepening past—the *longue durée* that is concerned with eternal man rather than individual figures—has also come under attack. Stuart Manning, whose work on chronology is of major significance, asserts that "the next great revolution in Aegean archaeology should, and will, be the active and urgent development of chronological precision on the order of an historical, individual- to generational-scale, resolution. . . . We can move from processual archaeology and broad datasets, to a humanistic, post-processual, archaeology. We can people prehistory."[63]

A notable example of the attempt to understand the role of people even in the *longue durée* is the Populus Project, begun in January 1994 with the goal of advancing "knowledge of European human demography in preindustrial times, c. 3000 BC–AD 1800." As the general editors contend, use of recently developed dating techniques should produce "more refined chronologies [that] seem likely to emphasize different rates of landscape change rather than uniformity, with profound implications for our understanding of human interactions with their landscape."[64]

We cannot eliminate the new directions in the human sciences, nor would we wish to. Quantification, which has been a major factor in the dehumanizing of history, can provide new insights. A recent publication by James H. Dee devotes more than six hundred pages to the examination of 1,269 epithets attached to personal names in the *Iliad* and *Odyssey*. One reviewer, Donald Lateiner, wonders that anyone would labor over, publish, distribute, or purchase such a study. Yet Lateiner concludes his appraisal with praise: "Dee has provided . . . the foundations for examining Homeric oral traditional poetry on the level of diction, metrics, composition, characterization, psychology, gender and class descriptors, repetition and originality." In providing this resource, "He has earned the gratitude of blind Homer, esteemed Demodocus and every student of Hellenic poetry."[65]

62. Lodge, *Thinks*, 319, 318; Pinker, *Blank Slate,* 48–49; Donald, *A Mind So Rare*, 200, 281, 300.

63. Manning, "From Process to People," 315, 322.

64. John Bintliff and Kostas Sbonias, eds., *Reconstructing Past Population Trends in Mediterranean Europe (3000 BC–AD 1800)*, ix.

65. Donald Lateiner, review of *Epitheta Hominum apud Homerum*, n.p.

However, the boundaries and subboundaries of the individual fields have become too rigid. The 1,269 epithets must be accessible to others who will use them to ask, and, one hopes, answer, other questions. As Braudel argues, "All the human sciences, history included, are affected by one another. They speak the same language, or could if they wanted to." There are welcome signs that the divisions are becoming more porous. In describing an archaeological project in New York State, David Wilson points to the "linking-up of archaeology and documentary history, so that at a crucial period one set of data illuminates, corrects and complements the other." He concludes his book with the optimistic observation that "if archaeology, and the new archaeology in particular with all its scientific alliances, are to expand on a large scale into those areas which have previously been the preserve of 'historical studies,' then the prospect is giddying indeed." In the nearly thirty years since Wilson suggested that prospect, significant progress has occurred in establishing interdisciplinary frameworks that link history and the natural and social sciences in a program of collaboration in fieldwork and colloquia. The Populus Project has the goal of learning more about European human demography stretching over forty-eight hundred years. Researchers include thirty British, four German, six Dutch, twenty-seven French, four Greek, thirty-five Italian, eight Slovenian, six Spanish, and eleven Canadian and U.S. scholars who "bridge the disciplinary and national boundaries that have mitigated against the development of a coherent methodology in Mediterranean Landscape archaeology."[66]

What of the challenge of relativism, that objects and texts have being only in individual interpretations of them? There is good news here, too. In his examination of human cognition that links the mind with culture, Merlin Donald makes a convincing case for ascribing meaning to words that goes well beyond an individual "reading" of meaning. "Every word is a cultural invention, and individuals must learn the consensual maps that every culture uses to graft word forms onto meanings." He speaks of the "tremendous pressure on the individual members of the founding group to adapt to the expanding language universe." Those meanings can be

66. Braudel, "Longue Durée," 34; Wilson, *The New Archaeology*, 336; Bintliff and Sbonias, *Past Population Trends*, iii, v.

learned even by those who are not part of the original culture: students of the human past endeavor to penetrate the cultures of particular points in the past by full attention to traces it has left behind. Even though the evidence is not complete, some succeed. John Bintliff offers a fine example of the reality of text in his paper in the first volume published by the Populus Project. Polybius, a historian from the second century BCE, observed that southern Greece was then suffering from depopulation. Given Polybius's view of the cyclical rise and fall of states, however, historians of antiquity doubt the accuracy of the observation. However, as Bintliff points out, "When intensive survey in Southern Greece found a widespread trend for the abandonment of rural farms and a parallel contraction in the occupied area of urban sites, Polybius and other early Roman era writers underwent a revolution." As for objects remaining from the past, Richard Brilliant has recently wrestled with the validity of interpreting the original meaning of objects remaining from the past in his book *My Laocoon*. He discusses his "sense of the persistence of a singular, material entity, the sculpture, in the face of diverging conceptual entities" and his presumption that "'something' exists in an objective state, prior to being interpreted." Just as bold, perhaps even bolder, is the argument of Ramsay MacMullen that it is possible to understand feelings and emotions in times long past.[67]

As early as 1982, M. J. Rowlands spoke of a "move back to a position implicitly or explicitly held by the founding ancestors of both the historical and social sciences."[68] This has not been the outcome. Rather, we see a rapprochement between the "old" and the "new." Scholars in the human sciences are no longer content to collect more and more data but have turned their attention to appropriate means of understanding those data. Individuals remain a favored subject of books and articles, but postmodern thought has shown the value of new areas and subjects, has demanded closer reading of texts, and has made scholars more critical of their own methods. We would be fools to disregard the aids of scientific technology. But we can honestly return to the subject of history: as Treischke declared, "Men [and women] make history."

67. Donald, *A Mind So Rare*, 291; Bintliff, "Regional Field Surveys and Population Cycles," in *Past Population Trends*, ed. Bintliff and Sbonias, 21; Brilliant, *My Laocoon: Alternative Claims in the Interpretation of Artworks*, 20, 30; MacMullen, *Feelings in History*.
68. Rowlands, "Processual Archaeology as Historical Social Science," 171.

In a careful discussion of the transformation of the study of Greek history, John Davies examines the "series of remarkable shifts and enlargements of scholarly focus, many of which have been heavily influenced by ideas and debates which have developed in other disciplines." His concluding words are cheering: "[A]ll forms of scholarship in Greek history . . . currently reflect a sense of confidence and innovative expansion."[69]

With two case studies of subjects taken from early Greek history, we will test this confidence and innovative approach. The first will consider Jason's quest for the Golden Fleece, a legacy from the "heroic" Bronze Age. The second will examine the poems of Hesiod, from the dawn of classical Greece, and test the substance of a claim that he is the first named figure in European history and one who describes his own world.

69. Davies, "Greek History: A Discipline in Transformation," 225, 246.

Launching the Argo

The story of the crisis of the human-related disciplines has brightened in the past few years, as many practicing them have realized that they cannot pattern their endeavors after the sciences, a realization due in no small measure to an awareness that their common subject was disappearing from view. Approaches adapted from the sciences produced general trends based on grand theories and compilations of statistical data. Use of highly technical tools led to narrow specialization that hampered cooperation not only among disciplines but within the disciplines themselves. Scholars studying the ancient world have been no more immune to this crisis than have humanists with other focuses, and like them they have lately begun a reconsideration of the challenges late-twentieth-century thinking has provided. In recent years, fragmentation and hostility have given way increasingly to accommodation.

Rather than becoming scientists, those engaged in the human-centered disciplines have increasingly appreciated the value of joining forces with scientists. The new juncture recognizes differences in disciplinary methods and goals but understands the potential inherent in cooperative enterprise. So great has been the progress that an age once described as having no place on land or sea is now set firmly in the Bronze Age as the first civilization of Greece. The value of scientific technology and methods has been acknowledged and incorporated into the search for evidence and subsequent study of the finds. New technology also assists our understanding of the human past by increasing the availability of essential information. Electronic technology has multiplied both the speed and the distance of regular communication among people, which has borne considerable fruit, and it is rewarding to note the growing cooperation among disciplines in large-scale projects aimed at understanding the human past. Nor is it simply the range of expertise that is joined; the casts of participants are increasingly international.

Finally, the inadequacy of extreme postmodern relativism has been detected. For preclassical Greece, the deconstruction aimed at objects was exceptionally restrictive since archaeological evidence provides the bulk of our information. While appreciating that the surviving material record of past cultures is limited, often impaired, and removed from its original context, archaeologists now look at physical objects in new ways, aided by scientific techniques of dating and analyzing composition of surviving artifacts. Objects become a window on the culture in which they existed, and they can, at times, shed light on the lives of individuals.

These and other recent developments not only have improved the well-being of history and related disciplines but also allow us to bring people into the picture of the past once again. The Greek Bronze Age provides a good case in point because it is a period lacking the kinds of sources needed to build a "systematic narrative of events and circumstances relating to man in his social or civil condition," the definition that *Webster's Unabridged Dictionary* assigns to history as a craft. Without that written narrative, we cannot discover the mental world of individual people or ever fully recover their lives. Yet I believe that the new spirit of cooperation among several related disciplines brings us much closer to particular, even named, inhabitants of the second millennium BCE. One such case is that of Jason who legendarily set sail from Iolkos in search of the Golden Fleece. The common belief about such a person journeying on such a voyage is shown in a recent *National Geographic* article on the Black Sea. The account begins with a reference to the tale of Jason's search for the Golden Fleece, supposedly hidden at the eastern end of that sea. "Jason never existed. And so he had to be invented," the account continues.[1] A number of clues suggest that this conclusion needs modification if not complete reversal.

---

1. Erla Zwingle, "Black Sea Coast: Crucible of the Gods," 80.

The Tale of Jason

Unlike many of the tales of the age of heroes, Jason's story is not an integral part of the story of Troy or the return of Odysseus after the Greek victory at Troy; rather, it centers on a figure named Jason whom some have found less than heroic. "Jason is scared of Medea," notes Peter Green, "but then Jason, at intervals, is scared of everything." Even so, he is bold enough to gather a group of companions from many parts of Greece, organize the construction of a ship, and sail off with his Argonauts to distant lands in search of the Golden Fleece. Even though not of the mold of Achilles and Odysseus, Jason belongs to the same heroic age, a time described even as late as 1938 as "a life that never was on land or sea. The men of [Homer's] time did not care to know; they were content to enter into and make their own a mythos of life." In fact, the story of Jason is found in most compilations of mythology—for instance, that of Edith Hamilton, who notes, "When the stories were being shaped, we are given to understand, little distinction had been made between the real and the unreal. The imagination was vividly alive and not checked by reason."[2]

This story begins in the kingdom of Iolkos, which had a troubled history. Its present king, Pelias, had seized the throne from the rightful heir, his half brother Aeson, whose father, Cretheus, had been the previous king. An oracle informed Pelias that he would be killed by a kinsman of Cretheus, a problem he solved by regularly putting to death any person resembling his half brother. When Aeson's wife gave birth to a child—obviously a blood relative of Cretheus—she wept over him as if the babe had been stillborn. Then, craftily, she had him smuggled out of the palace to Mount Pelion where he was raised by the centaur Cheiron.

Another oracle moved the tale forward in warning Pelias to especially beware of a man wearing only one sandal. One day he noticed a tall, long-haired young man wearing a single sandal. He had lost the other in carrying across a river an aged woman who in actuality was the goddess Hera come to punish Pelias for neglecting proper sacrifices to her. When Jason

---

2. Green, *Alexander to Actium: The Historical Evolution of the Hellenistic Age,* 210; Samuel Bassett, *The Poetry of Homer,* 244; Hamilton, *Mythology,* 13. Ian Morris gives a clear overview of changes in perceptions of early Greek history in *Archaeology and Cultural History: Words and Things in Iron Age Greece,* 77–106.

drew near, the king asked, "Who are you?" to which the young man re-plied that his foster father, the centaur, had called him Jason, son of Aeson. Not at all pleased, Pelias asked another somewhat peculiar question: "If an oracle announced to you," he said, "that one of your fellow-citizens was destined to kill you, what would you do?" Jason answered, "I would send him to fetch the golden ram's fleece from Colchis." In his turn, Jason asked the king who *he* was and, on learning that he was Pelias, straight-away demanded the throne. "Certainly," Pelias replied, "once you have re-covered the fleece of the divine ram that now hangs in a grove of trees, guarded by an unsleeping dragon."

That grove was near a remote kingdom named Colchis, located at the far end of the Black Sea. Magical means had brought the fleece to Colchis long before Jason's time, when a wonderful ram with fleece of gold had been sent by Hermes to rescue two children about to be sacrificed. The ram snatched them up, carrying them far away on his back. The girl, Helle, fell off over a strait of water destined to bear her name—Helles-pont—but the boy was safely conveyed to Colchis where he was kindly received by its king. In gratitude for his rescue, the boy sacrificed the ram to Zeus as a thanks offering. Its fleece was preserved as a great treasure.

This was the fleece that Pelias ordered Jason to recover. Jason accepted the charge, but realizing that he needed companions, he sent heralds throughout Greece calling for volunteers. He prevailed on one Argus to build a fifty-oared ship, bearing the name *Argo,* for the enterprise. Athena herself fitted a beam into the prow of the ship from wood cut from her father Zeus's oak tree at Dodona. The tale of the *Argonautica* recounts the adventures and misadventures of the crew, most of whom—though not all—reached their destination at the eastern edge of the Black Sea, liber-ated the fleece, and fled, with the help of Medea, the daughter of the king of Colchis.

All the ingredients that regularly find their way onto a list of character-istics of myth are present: divinities, nondivine but certainly nonhuman creatures, interaction between gods and mortals, oracles, remoteness from the present, and lively entertainment.[3] In addition, the tale wears the mask

---

3. John Chadwick, unpublished paper given to author, "Some Thoughts on Greek Myths."

of history since threads of proper names of people and places and events are woven into its fabric, although its authorship is unknown. It is no wonder that early Greek history was seen as a flight of imagination, a fabrication, when tales like the *Argonautica* and the Trojan War supplied the only evidence.

What makes its historical value even less credible is the fact that the full tale is later than the classical age of Greek history; it is the written creation of Apollonius of Rhodes, who lived in the third century BCE. The poem is a hexameter epic akin to the *Iliad* and *Odyssey*, and its content draws heavily on that of the earlier epics. The group of heroes gathered for the quest resembles the Achaean leaders and counselors at Troy, and Jason and his men must do battle against a slew of enemies. In their struggles they are aided considerably by the gods: for example, Athena intervenes to push the *Argo* through the Clashing Rocks. So abhorrent to Zeus is the slaughter of Apsyrtus, the son and heir of the king of Colchis, that he punishes the Argonauts with wanderings that rival, if not surpass, those of Odysseus and his men.

Although related in genre and general theme to the *Iliad* and *Odyssey* that many date in their final form to the eighth century, the *Argonautica* belongs to its own age of composition, the cosmopolitan Hellenistic age founded in the wake of the conquests of Alexander the Great of Macedon. Apollonius of Rhodes seems to have been born in Alexandria in Egypt, where he served as director of the huge library of the Ptolemies; it is only through self-imposed exile to Rhodes that he gained his cognomen. (That exile was taken, it is said, due to the disastrous reception of his epic recounting of the voyage of the *Argo*.)

Most modern scholars are of the opinion expressed by Robin Lane Fox that the *Argonautica* is "less an epic than an intermittent display of gifts common in the best Hellenistic poets." Apollonius's poem shows the characteristics of Alexandrian poetry, not those of the earlier epics. The content, too, shows knowledge possessed by Hellenistic Greeks but absent in the late Dark Age and Archaic Age: the precision of the ship's itinerary, details of ship construction and handling by the crew, and geographical certainty. So exact are such details that the poem "may be read on one level as a collection of aetiological and geographical data on various Mediterranean and Black Sea locations, even as a treatise on navigational routes."[4] By contrast, identification of routes of the Greeks sailing to and home from Troy has exercised the imaginations of a good many minds. The collective effort has produced no generally accepted route plan, for how does one identify the islands of the Cyclopes, Circe, and the king of the winds?

Another contribution from the Hellenistic age is the poet's exploration of character, not only of humans but also of deities and animals. Not awe but pathos and often dread are the responses that arise from accounts of Medea's weeping in silence while her heart is bursting, the Argonauts' frequent bouts of despair, and the sad creatures of ill-assorted limbs gathered about Circe whom Jason and Medea meet on their long journey back to Greece. So prominent are these probings that one translator of the poem believed that Apollonius "was certainly abreast of all the scientific movements of his day, and probably ahead of some of them, as for instance in the field of what we now call abnormal psychology."[5]

The features deriving from its mythical framework and Hellenistic composition distance the evidence even further from its purported place and period of reference in the second millennium BCE. However, a great deal of information derived from a variety of tools has joined the evidence of such tales as the *Voyage of the Argo* to make them—possibly—more than flights of imagination, set in the fictitious setting of a "heroic" age. Discussing the new evidence will serve not only to test the historical value of the adventures of Jason and his crew but also to demonstrate the prospect

---

4. Fox, "Hellenistic Culture and Literature," 359. On the characteristics, see Green, *Alexander to Actium*, 205. In comparing the poetry of Callimachus and Apollonius, Green states, "What both poets in fact reveal is an identical, and ineradicable, Alexandrianism, with its twin temptations of scholarship and naïveté, which emerges as a kind of social index and correlative" (205). Not all are of this opinion, however. C. Pietsch, in *Die Argonautika des Apollonios von Rhodes*, argues that the poem shows continuity rather than a break with the earlier epic tradition. On the exactness of details, see R. J. Clare, "Epic Itineraries: The Sea and Seafaring in the *Odyssey* of Homer and the *Argonautica* of Apollonius Rhodius," 6.

5. E. V. Rieu, trans., *The Voyage of Argo*, 23. Rieu's introduction is sympathetic to the poet and his poem, setting both within the context of the poet's own time. As he concludes his comments, Rieu adds, "So far, this essay has been devoted to a just appraisal of Apollonius' merits and to rebutting his detractors. Now, I must in all honesty add a few criticisms of my own" (30).

of finding individual people in early Greece. For the first goal, we must establish correspondence among places, peoples, and technological skills described in the written account of the *Argonautica* with evidence that now exists for the heroic age. Then, if appropriate places, peoples, and skills are attested for preclassical Greece, we can ask whether the three categories of evidence converge in time. If so, it is possible to propose that the tale goes back to an Ur-*Argonautica* dating to as much as a millennium earlier than the time of Apollonius of Rhodes.

Recent Developments in Archaeology

Because textual evidence is limited for Bronze Age Greece, we begin with contributions of archaeology, especially those associated with its "coming-of-age" in the second half of the twentieth century. Until roughly 1950, the task of archaeologists was to discover and then uncover evidence of past cultures. Their main tools were shovels and strong arms. After recovering objects, their task was to apply rigorous analysis of the material remains in order to reconstruct a picture of the life of people who produced and used them. As a result of successful excavation, evidence increased to a point that it could be overwhelming, one of the contributors to the reassessment of the discipline described in "History at the Crossroads."

However, it did not overturn the view of many, like Samuel Bassett, that the Greek age of heroes has no place in history. A dramatic shift in opinion occurred in the generation from about 1940 to 1970, when the pace of new discoveries and new theories increased in a mysterious geometric progression. Especially altered was the definition of the age of heroes. James T. Hooker introduced his 1976 study of Mycenaean Greece with the declaration, "I propose . . . to discuss, from a historical point of view, some of the crucial periods in the development of Aegean lands during the Bronze Age."[6] A number of developments in the discipline of archaeology enabled this enormous shift of opinion.

First to occur was the discovery of a larger number of sites and a greater range of material evidence. Pioneer archaeologists seeking evidence of the Bronze Age in the Aegean succeeded in revealing a few often isolated sites. Heinrich Schliemann, for example, excavated productively at Hissarlik (now

6. Hooker, *Mycenaean Greece*, 1.

generally acknowledged to be the location of Troy) and at Mycenae (which every reader of the *Iliad* knew as the home of Agamemnon), Orchomenos, and Tiryns. However, these few sites, whose dating was initially unclear, did not constitute a broadly based or chronologically fixed culture. In the twentieth century, a brace of new discoveries throughout the Aegean sphere provided a picture of widespread culture with similarities between the artifacts of individual sites demonstrating the interactive character of that culture. This dimension of archaeology continues today.

Consequently, archaeologists now appreciate the importance of a regional perspective, rather than focusing solely on single impressive sites. Moreover, survey archaeology shifts attention from major centers where rulers dwelled and administered their realms to the domain of ordinary people spread throughout the region to achieve its goal of investigating the relationship between the land and its use by people. Accompanying this development is an expanded membership in the investigation: because the goal of survey archaeology is so broad, a variety of specialists join forces. Archaeologists work with geographers, geologists, engineers, economists, historians, and linguists to understand the evidence they recover.

Related to this cooperation of specialists is the integration of new technologies into the discipline of archaeology. The current tool kit includes magnetometers that reveal features beneath the earth's surface and objects buried in the seafloor, robots for investigating caves inaccessible to humans, tools of aerial reconnaissance, and, of course, computers. Dates can be learned through many techniques, from radiocarbon and dendrochronology to analysis of charged atoms. Pots are now tested to reveal the composition of their clay. Such tools give access to evidence previously unattainable, while the analysis of the evidence allows more precise conclusions on such important subjects as dating and the origin of materials and thus patterns of exchange both within the Aegean and beyond.

A view beyond the Aegean is essential to the transformation of archaeology from a discipline that relied primarily on shovels and strong arms. In the early days of archaeology, study of single sites or regional cultures was sufficiently demanding and arduous work, but that focus produced isolated snapshots, not a broad panorama. The wider perspective of the past three decades or so has located the Aegean within its larger contemporary context of the Mediterranean and even more distant societies. It is now clear that Bronze Age cultures, particularly in the eastern Mediterranean but also farther away, were interactive. To be sure, the individual cultures were marked by distinct characteristics, nor were the participants in the interactive network drawn into a single political unit. Even so, that interlocking network must be taken into account to understand the individual histories of the participants.

The broader view has lengthened chronological horizons of what has been called "archaeography," that is, the writing of history through its archaeological evidence.[7] Until recently, many historians saw little connection between the Bronze Age culture currently being unearthed and that of classical Greece. But with the decipherment of the Linear B script as an early form of Greek, the division between the two periods narrowed. Continuities demonstrated in the material culture now reveal common elements reaching a millennium earlier than the "golden age" of classical Greece.[8] With the demonstration of continuity, accounts from the classical, literate world reflecting on the "age of heroes" may merit greater trust than they were accorded in the past.

One negative feature of the discipline arising during the perceived crisis in archaeology in the 1960s has, happily, abated. We have seen that akin to the other disciplines concerned with the human past, archaeology became a target of critical theory informed by the relativism inherent in deconstructionism and postmodernism. According to this position, the traces of the past that persist belong to a time other than the present. Because it is impossible to live in the past and thus experience it directly, a person living in another time cannot truly know the past. Furthermore, each person confronting the past allies his or her own distinct perspectives, values, and goals to the evidence. Consequently, the reconstruction of that evidence will reflect these differences rather than any sense of an original purpose or function.

A significant factor in reestablishing the possibility of gaining information from surviving artifacts has been the emergence of tools and ap-

7. François Hartog, *Memories of Odysseus: Frontier Tales from Ancient Greece* (originally published as *Memoire d'Ulysse* [Paris: Éditions Gallimard, 1996]), 58.

8. Especially valuable is Roland Hampe and Erika Simon, *The Birth of Greek Art: From the Mycenaean to the Archaic Period.*

proaches that enhance the quality of information that physical objects can provide. Object biography is one of the most exciting of these perspectives. The basic premise of this approach is that objects, like people, are transformed over time, not simply in physical ways but also in their uses and value. As dating techniques have been sharpened, it is possible to follow the lifeline of, say, a clay pot. Made for a particular function, it can become a gift to a friend that is now valued for its connection to a person rather than simply for its function. Even if it is removed from its place of origin, analysis of its clay can assist in locating its first location and thereby describe connections between areas. So great may its value become that it later serves as a prize in a competition. Finally, on the death of the victor of that competition, the pot is buried with him as a mark of his honor. Linked with this premise is the view that changes in objects are linked to changes in the lives of people.

Some physical remains proved to offer written evidence once the mysterious symbols incised on certain clay tablets were deciphered in the early 1950s. Their contents were shown to be accounts of people, livestock, products, and events as recorded by scribes in the service of the central authority of several of the kingdoms.[9] The accounts are short, statistical records; consequently, they are hardly the basis of genuine historical accounts. However, those records were administrative tools created and kept in the citadel centers of large regional kingdoms. Not only has the script of the tablets on the Greek mainland—known as the Linear B tablets—been deciphered as an early form of Greek, but ongoing study of the contents has displayed minute details in the lives of certain people living during a single year of the late Bronze Age. Thus, these "laundry lists" provide concrete evidence previously absent from the available sources. In a moment we will consider their value to the case of an Ur-*Argonautica*.

Archaeology in the Case of an Ur-*Argonautica*

The service to historical reconstruction of tools now at our disposal can be tested in the case of Jason and his Argonauts to learn whether the tradition is more than a mythos. We must begin at the first stage in the emergence of

9. Tablets do not exist for all of the kingdoms; the major sources are Pylos, Knossos, Mycenae, Tiryns, and Thebes.

Aegean archaeography, that is, with Heinrich Schliemann, who set the goal of demonstrating the historical reality of another event of the "legendary" past, the Trojan War. To achieve his goal, he knew he must locate certain sites: Troy for one and Mycenae for another. By uncovering both, he hoped to prove the reality of a civilization that until then was thought to be no more than the product of the lively Greek imagination. Even in spite of his startling results, many remained unconvinced. W. A. Stillman, an archaeologist contemporary with Schliemann, stated in the London *Times* (on January 9, 1889): "I hope before long to put all the evidence . . . in such a shape that no one can doubt reasonably that 'Troy' is the Troy of Croesus [that is, the sixth century BCE] and Tiryns a Byzantine palace of about 1000 A.D." Others were not persuaded that Schliemann's excavated site had a connection with any age of true history: Troy could be found not in the trenches of Hissarlik, but only among the Muses who dwell on Olympus.

Even this amateur archaeologist seeking the site of Troy recognized that evidence from more than a single site or two was needed: material remains from one location might be remarkable, yet they would be without a context, either chronological or cultural. To provide this larger context, Schliemann excavated not only at Troy and Mycenae but also at Tiryns and Orchomenos. He made soundings on the islands of Kythera and Ithaka, also in the area of the Peloponnese where Pylos, the kingdom of Nestor, was traditionally situated, and on Crete. The next generation of archaeologists would follow his example, revealing sophisticated Bronze Age cultures throughout the Aegean region. Impressive palace centers on the Greek mainland were uncovered at Pylos, Mycenae, Tiryns, Midea, Athens, Thebes, Gla, Orchomenos, and, most recently, in the Northeast, near the modern town of Volos. Volos leads us back to Jason.

Trial excavations at Volos in Thessaly occurred in the summer of 1956 at a site identified at the turn of the century as dating to the Bronze Age. This midcentury investigation produced confirmation of that identification in the form of settlement from about 2500 to 1200 BCE.[10] Subsequent exploration has shown that during the late Bronze Age the site was dominated by two successive large buildings, akin to the buildings at better-

10. See Demetrios R. Theochares, "Iolkos: Whence Sailed the Argonauts."

known locations such as Mycenae and Pylos that are described as palaces. The first building dates to the fifteenth century BCE; it continued in use through the fourteenth century into the thirteenth when it was rebuilt. Large rooms with fresco fragments and stuccoed floors, fine bronze weapons, rich burials, and a large tholos tomb led to the conclusion that this was the northernmost of the major centers of Mycenaean Greece, known through legend as Iolkos. That the settlement was not a remote outlier but rather had direct contact with the southern Mycenaean centers is shown by the pottery collected there, much of which was imported.

Appreciation of the importance of the northern area of the nearby bay of Pagasai has lately increased even more. Excavations in 2001 at the site of Dimini, just west of the site believed to be Iolkos, have revealed two parts of a large building that covered some seven thousand square yards. The building, which Vasiliki Ardymi-Sismani of the Greek ministry of culture terms a palace, is large (the total complex is about fifty-two hundred square meters), and it contains two large megara connected by an internal court (about sixteen hundred square meters). Although it is early in the

Walls of Iolkos as pictured in 1958.

investigation, the building appears to have served the same purposes that more southern centers incorporated: it was a storage and production hub as well as a residence. The presence of clay baths together with a system for water drainage indicates the same sophisticated technology apparent in other Mycenaean centers. Excavations also produced traces of a wide thoroughfare passing between houses surrounding the palace. Previously known from nearby Dimini are two large tholos tombs that, though robbed, still contained some remains of gold and glass jewelry.[11] An announcement in the Greek newspaper *Kathimerini* on February 10, 2004, reported the find of an intact, apparently unplundered Mycenaean tholos on the ring road around Volos. *Ta Nea* on June 7, 2004, announced the discovery of four pit graves covered with slabs; one excavated grave contained remains of humans and animals together with pottery, gold necklace beads, semiprecious stones, and weapons. It is dated to the fourteenth century BCE.

The value of the new evidence extends beyond a single site; it adds considerably to our understanding of the larger region. Although reconnaissance of the terrain was one of the earliest practices of students of antiquity, the technique of surveying a more extensive region has been enriched with more precise methods and more specific goals. The discovery of major centers in itself encouraged careful study of the regions surrounding those focal points. Thus, we can and should examine the nature of southeastern Thessaly.

Iolkos is located on a high mound (approximately 400 by 270 meters) overlooking both the Gulf of Pagasai and the Volos plain; Dimini is situated on a mound on a low spur projecting into that same plain, the fertility of which has made Thessaly one of the main centers of agricultural production since the Neolithic period.[12] Both features are characteristic of the Mycenaean citadel centers that have been more thoroughly studied. Combining the topography with other evidence, which we will consider directly, produces an economic picture in which control of agriculture and livestock provided the foundation for growing specialization throughout an expanding region under the citadels' control. In both the *Iliad* and the

11. Information from http://www.enet.gr/online/online_pl_text.jsp?c=113&id=88688 (March 8, 2002).

12. Richard Hope Simpson, *Mycenaean Greece*, 161–63.

Odyssey, livestock figures prominently in references to Thessaly: King Pelias was rich in sheep (*Od.* 11.256–57); in the catalog of the Achaeans at Troy, some hailed from Thessalian Iton, the mother of sheep (*Il.* 2.696), and the warrior Eumelos, who led the Thessalian contingent from Pherai, Boibe, Glaphyria, and Iolkos, is, by his name, abounding in sheep (*Il.* 2.711–14).

An even more expansive regional picture emerges by inserting Iolkos into the larger Mycenaean world, one that was connected by direct contact. In fact, the very emergence of the Mycenaean civilization rested upon this contact. As James Hooker puts the case, "The evolution in Messenia and in the Argolid, of a homogeneous Mycenaean culture can have taken place only in a context of trade-routes which linked different parts of Greece with the outside world and with one another." Pottery is key evidence; not only apparent similarities in design and decoration but also composition of the clay through recent technological analysis demonstrates the movement of vessels and the contents they once contained.[13] Pottery found in the Volos region of Thessaly during the middle Bronze Age (roughly 2100–1600 BCE) came from central Greece, the northeastern Peloponnese, the island of Aegina, and the Cycladic islands. Examples from the late Bronze Age show kinship with pictorial pottery from centers such as Mycenae, Tiryns, Athens, and Lefkandi.[14] Moreover, parallels between Iolkos and other Mycenaean sites in the physical organization of the palace and its relation to smaller houses express cultural homogeneity.

So, thus far, we have a site dated to the Bronze Age whose main building compares with structures in southern Greece described as palaces, and burials suggest the architectural form and richness of objects found in other Bronze Age sites. Mycenaean features place the site within the larger Greek culture of the second millennium BCE. However, if we are to locate a "Jason" within this scenario, Iolkos must be associated with the wider Aegean sphere and even beyond, to the eastern edge of the Black Sea.

13. Hooker, *Mycenaean Greece,* 57. For instance, the analysis of clay from pottery found at Thebes demonstrates that its fabric is comparable with the fabric of pottery from Crete (H. W. Catling and A. Millett, "A Study of the Inscribed Stirrup-Jars from Thebes," 35).

14. On pottery from other parts of Greece, see Stelios Andreou, Michael Fotiadis, and Kostas Kotsakis, "Aegean Prehistory V: The Neolithic and Bronze Age of Northern Greece." On pictorial kinship, see Sara A. Immerwahr, "Some Pictorial Fragments from Iolkos."

Bronze Age Seafaring

Not only is the use of seacraft being pushed earlier and earlier, but certain regions are now seen as "potential nurseries for the development of maritime technology and navigation."[15] Even before the Bronze Age, travel by sea in the Aegean is clearly attested. Ships brought the first settlers to the island of Crete about 6000 BCE, and those settlers continued to rely on the sea for purposes of trade. Ships also carried the first settlers to the islands of the Aegean known as the Cyclades about 4300 BCE. It is increasingly clear that lively interaction existed within the Aegean from as early as the late fourth and early third millennia. Initially, settlers in the Cyclades employed their longships, developed around 3000 BCE, to gain goods unavailable on their rocky homes in trade for their own crafts, like elegant marble vessels and sculptures, and goods such as olive oil and wine. These seafarers moved among the islands and beyond them to other parts of the Aegean. Excavations in the summer of 2001 uncovered remains of a flourishing, fortified settlement on the southwestern coast of Andros dating to around 4500–3300 BCE. There the excavator Christina Televantou discovered incised pictures of ten ships between twenty and thirty centimeters in length on the outer face of the defensive wall as well as two ships on the wall's rock foundations. And sailors appear to have reached the eastern Mediterranean. The Carmel mountain ridge in the Levant has a number of incised pictures of boats of various forms and sizes. One boat, dated to the Neolithic period, is an Aegean type of vessel.[16]

Inhabitants of Crete soon expanded this incipient trade in the Aegean, where "thousands of imported vases (the great majority from Crete)" show Minoan presence.[17] Locations in Anatolia, too, reveal that same presence through objects and, in several cases, through actual settlements. Well beyond the Aegean, Minoan goods and influence were felt in Egypt, the Levant, and the central Mediterranean. Somewhat later, inhabitants of mainland Greece involved themselves in this intensive network of trade during the

15. C. Paul Rainbird, "Islands Out of Time: Towards a Critique of Island Archaeology," 231.

16. See M. Artzy, "Routes, Trade, Boats, and 'Nomads of the Sea.'"

17. Malcolm Wiener, "The Isles of Crete? The Minoan Thalassocracy Revisited," 135.

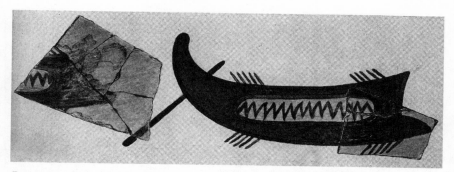

Reconstruction of a ship painted on a potsherd from Iolkos dating to the first half of the second millennium.

second half of the second millennium. Increasing presence of mainland goods, and surely mainlanders, extends eastward from the Aegean islands to the Anatolian coast and neighboring islands, southward to Crete, and on to Egypt and the Levant.[18] Even before these eastern interests, Mycenaeans had been active in the central Mediterranean, as finds from southern Italy and Sicily demonstrate.

To argue that trade was a common activity within the Mycenaean world does not demonstrate that Iolkos was a regular participant. On the other hand, goods from other areas tell us that this part of Thessaly was at least on the receiving end of trade and that there were sufficient goods to draw traders to the Gulf of Pagasai. And by the middle of the second millennium, pottery fragments from the area of Iolkos itself are decorated with a series of many-oared boats. Seafaring, then, was not foreign to the mentality of those living near Iolkos during the age of heroes. Thus, we can feel reasonably secure in putting some Thessalian Mycenaeans on boats in the second millennium. But can we send any of those boats into the Black Sea?

In the early days of Aegean archaeology, Walter Leaf proposed that

18. On the Aegean islands, see R. L. N. Barber, "The Mycenaeans and the Cyclades." On Anatolia, see C. Mee, "Anatolia and the Aegean in the Late Bronze Age." On Egypt, see R. Merrilles, "Egypt and the Aegean." On the Levant, see A. Killebrew, "Mycenaean and Aegean-Type Pottery in Canaan during the 14th–12th Centuries BC." See also Eric H. Cline, *Sailing the Wine-Dark Sea: International Trade in the Late Bronze Age Aegean*, and his Web site, http://home.gwu/75%ehcline/CLINEDB.htm.

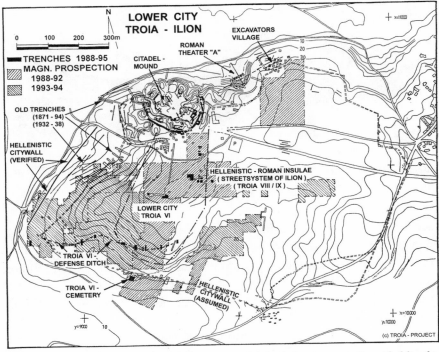

The citadel and lower town of Troy shown through magnetometry. Provided by the editor of the Internet presentation of the Troia-Project.

Troy's importance was due to its location, which controlled access to the Propontis and, thence, to the Black Sea. Though not widely adopted, the view persisted and has been enlivened by recent study of the area surrounding the citadel at Hissarlik-Troy. In 1988, Manfred Korfmann, of the University of Tübingen, was granted a license to begin new excavations at Troy; since that date, German archaeologists have worked in conjunction with a team of archaeologists from the University of Cincinnati. During the summer season, approximately one hundred specialists come to the site in this international and interdisciplinary project that blends specialized scientific technologies with traditional archaeological goals. Their results are as impressive as their procedures. Investigation during the past decade has revealed a city of several thousand inhabitants living in a town at the foot of the citadel excavated by Schliemann. The extent of the town is now gauged to be some forty-five acres, compared with the five acres enclosed by the citadel walls. The occupants engaged in lively trade with a range of other cultures and actively produced goods, especially metal objects, for that trade.[19]

Unhappily, but not unexpectedly in archaeography, the new findings at the site have triggered an angry debate. Whereas the excavators argue that results demonstrate that Troy was an important commercial center with a population of five thousand to ten thousand residents, critics (particularly the historians Frank Kolb and Karl-Joachim Hölkeskamp and the archaeologist Henner von Hesberg) assert that no such conclusion is possible based on the findings. Instead, they maintain that the Bronze Age site at Troy was a small village and, in fact, lacked a harbor.[20]

Again, the incorporation of sophisticated scientific technologies into archaeological research offers an answer. A group of specialists has provided a revised view of the Trojan region: since 1980, hydrologists have been working to reconstruct the configuration of the ancient site. The many apparent discrepancies between the Homeric description and its present topography shrink, if they do not completely disappear, with recent findings. One important conclusion is that the bay between Sigeium and Cape Rhoetum (the western and eastern points of entrance into the bay) was considerably deeper and larger in the second millennium BCE than it is at present. Over the centuries, silting has made it shallower and less extensive. Thus, ships, even a fleet, could have sailed into a harbor at the front door of the settlement rather than anchoring or beaching miles away, as

19. See Leaf, *Troy: A Study in Homeric Geography.* For a detailed description of the plan of Troy as of 1998, see J. V. Luce, *Celebrating Homer's Landscapes: Troy and Ithaca Revisited.* Mikhail Treister, in "The Trojan Treasures: Description, Chronology, Historical Context," reasons that the treasures help to reveal the status of Troy as an important participant in trade as early as the third millennium. James C. Wright concludes, "As Professor Korfmann has eloquently demonstrated . . . during the entire bronze age, Troy was a gatekeeper between the Aegean and the Black Sea" ("The Place of Troy among the Civilizations of the Bronze Age," 49).

20. Useful articles about the current debate are Rüdiger Heimlich, "The New Trojan Wars," and an interview with Wolf-Dietrich Niemeier, "Greeks vs. Hittites: Why Troy Is Troy and the Trojan War Is Real." Opposing the stated results is H.-J. Behr, G. Biegel, and H. Castritius, eds., *Traum und Wirklichkeit: Troia: Ein Mythos in Geschichte und Rezeption.*

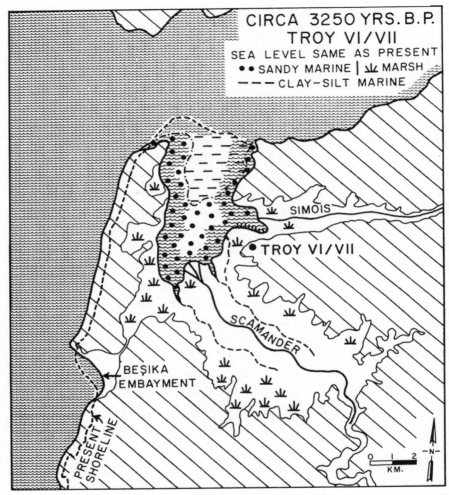

Paleogeographic reconstruction of the vicinity of Troy around 3250 BP. (Courtesy of the Department of Classics, University of Cincinnati)

the topography is now configured. From the bay near Troy, a series of linked beaches stretched northward to the Hellespont. The reconstructed configuration places the Greek camp westward across the bay from Troy, instead of along the coast north of the citadel, as most earlier plans had imagined. The director of the study of the city, Manfred Korfmann, views

Troy as an anchorage for ships waiting for favorable conditions to sail eastward.[21]

Mycenaean ships may not have been in that anchorage, yet it is worthwhile to draw upon a source made more plausible by the recognition that Greek history reaches well before 776 BCE. The *Iliad* remembers that Euneos, a son of Jason, sent ships from his island home of Lemnos, bringing wine to the Achaeans at Troy for which they exchanged bronze, iron, hides, whole oxen, and slaves (7.473–75). And even if Greek ships were not to be found in the harbor, a Mycenaean presence at Troy is clearly attested by archaeological finds. Mycenaean objects at Troy begin in the sixteenth century and continue into the thirteenth. As we have noted, Mycenaean goods are also found at many sites along the coast of Anatolia; a former Minoan settlement at Miletus seems to have become "Mycenaean" in the middle range of the millennium. Goods also moved from east to west, and, for our present inquiry, particular interest attaches to the Anatolian link of pottery present at the site of Pefkakia near Iolkos-Volos at the end of the third millennium.[22]

More significant in a search for a voyage of the *Argo,* goods from the Aegean sphere increasingly are being identified in the Propontis and even in the Black Sea itself. Mycenaean pottery has been at found Masat, 130 kilometers inland from the south coast of the Black Sea. Rapiers, spear heads, and double axes, which are either imports or imitations of Aegean types, show contact between Thrace and the Aegean. One hundred fifty stone anchors discovered mainly off Cape Kaliakra and two ox-hide ingots betray an Aegean impact; one copper ingot bears an incised mark comparable to the linear signs used on Crete and mainland Greece. In the north of the Black Sea, harnessing accessories have come to light, and cheek pieces in this find are virtually identical to two pairs of cheek pieces from the shaft graves at Mycenae. And from the eastern Black Sea, long swords are "relatives" to Mycenaean examples. Reverse contact from the Black Sea to Greece is also suggested in the boars' tusk helmets, arrow smoothers, horse burials, and the source of gold found in the shaft graves. Analysis of

21. See J. C. Kraft, I. Kayan, and O. Erol, "Geomorphic Reconstructions in the Environs of Ancient Troy"; Kraft, "Geology and Paleogeographic Reconstructions of the Vicinity of Troy"; and Korfmann, "Troy: Topography and Navigation."

22. Andreou, Fotiadis, and Kotsakis, "Aegean Prehistory V," 269.

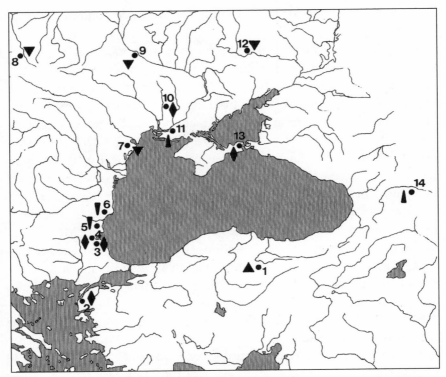

Aegean finds in the Black Sea. The symbols are: diamond = double axe; down-pointed wedge = ingot; up-pointed wedge = weapon; pyramid = ceramic; and down-pointed pyramid = bone. (With permission of Robert Laffineur, ed., Thalassa: L'Egeo prehistorique et la mer [Liège: University of Liège, 1991], pl. 58)

gold found at Mycenae shows that it is of the type free of tin and platinum that has also been found at Varna on the Bulgarian coast of the Black Sea.[23]

The evidence derived from archaeology also provides a larger perspective in attesting to a flourishing civilization in Greece during the heroic age that participated with other cultures in the interactive trade. The inventory of goods found with a fourteenth-century ship wrecked off the south-

---

23. The information on finds is from Stephan Hillar, "The Mycenaeans and the Black Sea." For the analysis of gold, see James Muhly, "Gold Analysis and Sources of Gold in the Bronze Age," 3–4.

ern coast of Turkey is proof of this trade's international character: the inventory includes pottery from Cyprus and Syria-Palestine; metal goods of Egyptian, Cypriot, Canaanite, and Mycenaean design; Canaanite glass; a cylinder seal from the Kassite kingdom; beads of Baltic amber; an Egyptian hieroglyphic scarab bearing the name of Nefertiti; two hippopotamus teeth; a length of elephant tusk; fragments of tortoiseshell; and a small folded tablet of wood. The picture that such a wealth of objects calls up is port-to-port voyaging, with goods traded and added at each new landing. Iolkos is part of this picture. Thus, we have appropriate real places: Iolkos in mainland Greece and Mycenaean goods in the sea where the *Argo* was said to have sailed. One of the lures may well have been gold for which the Thessalians could have traded fine cloth. Morris Silver concludes that "it is possible to entertain the hypothesis that the underlying meaning of the Argonaut myth is that the Argo arrived in Kolchis with a cargo of purple-dyed cloth and returned to Iolkos with their price in gold. In this sense, the ship carried the 'golden Fleece' to the Black Sea and returned to Greece with the 'Golden Fleece.'"[24]

Philology

Archaeology does not stand unaided in a quest for the Golden Fleece. Philology, the study of words and speech, provides independent testimony. Joining the two disciplines should make a stronger case, if philology has anything at all to contribute. To anticipate, it has several contributions to add, particularly about people.

The first clue is that Jason, the *Argo,* and the adventures of the Argonauts were known far earlier than the third century. Working backward in time from Apollonius, fragments remain of the poetry of one Antimachos, who wrote in the early fourth century; several of those fragments relate to the Argonaut tale. Euripides' tragedy *Medea* is dated to 431. Pindar (518–438) told the story of Jason in his Fourth Pythian Ode, and the lyric poet Mimnermus, who flourished around 600 BCE, described Jason's goal as

24. See G. F. Bass et al., "The Bronze Age Shipwreck at Ulu Burun: 1986 Campaign, 1–29"; and Silver's Web site, "Ancient Economies I," topic 5, "The Argonaut Epos and Bronze Age Economic History," http://members.tripod.com/~sondmor/index-4.html, p. 4 of printed copy.

Aia, at the edge of Ocean. Eumelus, who lived in the seventh century, linked Medea, who followed Jason from Colchis to Greece, with both Iolkos and Corinth. One of the earliest references is also one of the most enticing: in book 12 of the *Odyssey*, Circe, in giving Odysseus advice about his journey away from her island, mentions the one ship—the widely sung *Argo*—that escaped the perilous sea awaiting him. Ahead of the *Argo*

> There stand the jutting rocks and before them resounds
> The mighty wave of dark-browed Amphitrite.
> The blessed gods call them the Clashing Rocks.
> No birds, not even the timid doves who bring
> Ambrosia to Father Zeus can pass them by.
> But the sheer face of rock always catches them
> And the Father must add another to fill the cohort.
> No ships of men can escape this place, if any should even
>   reach it.
> But the salty waves and fiery winds carry away
> The timbers of ships and bodies of men, all mixed together.
> Yet one seafaring ship sailed through them,
> The far-famed Argo returning from the land of Aietes.
> It was Hera who helped it pass since Jason was dear to her.
>   (59–72)

As mentioned previously, the *Iliad* mentions Euneos, the son of Jason, who brought wine to the Achaeans from Lemnos (7.467–68). This same Euneos paid a ransom to redeem Lykaon, one of Priam's sons (21.41–42). The ransom took the form of a silver mixing bowl that later became a prize in the funeral games for Patroklos (23.746–48). Hesiod, too, recounts the union of Jason, son of Aison, and Medea, daughter of Aietes (*Theogony* 992–1002).

This range of references informs us that a tale of the *Argo* was known in the archaic and classical ages; in other words, it was not created in the Hellenistic world. It was familiar to Hesiod, who can be quite securely dated to the end of the eighth century, and to "Homer"—or a bard by another name who sang the tales of the Trojan War—perhaps around the mid-eighth century. We can move even further back in time if, in company with many people, we believe the poems of Hesiod and Homer have deep roots in an enduring oral tradition.

Almost everything associated with the name of Homer has been debated hotly since antiquity. In his *Vera Historia,* dating to the second century CE, Lucian describes an imaginary interview that he had with the poet in which Homer said, "As a matter of fact, I am a Babylonian, and among my fellow-countrymen my name was not Homer but Tigranes. Later on, when I was a hostage *(homeros)* among the Greeks, I changed by name" (*II.* 20). Debate and speculation lasting through the centuries prompted William Mure to write in the nineteenth century, "During five and twenty hundred years this inquiry has occupied the subtlest investigators of every age. On no other similar subject have more strange or conflicting theories been proposed, more voluminous commentaries expended, or a keener spirit of controversy displayed; on none, perhaps, has the lavish exuberance of speculative inquiry been more barren hitherto of positive results."[25] Such lavish exuberance of speculative inquiry points in four major directions: Homer's "identity," the authorship of the two epics, the historical basis of the poems, and the nature of the epic language.

It is the fourth question that concerns us here, especially the recent understanding of the nonliterate basis of the language of the Homeric epics. Essentially, the debate centers on the mixture of dialects in the language of the poems, a mixture that apparently had no historical counterpart. Certain linguists argue that the language was a spoken language at one time, resulting from the existence in one community of people speaking several different dialects of Greek. Others maintain that it never was a spoken language; rather, the mix stemmed from the fact that the poems were first composed in one dialect and later transcribed into another. Another hypothesis is that the language was completely artificial, a literary creation.

The American classicist Milman Parry offered another solution in the 1920s in demonstrating the role of oral tradition in the creation of epic literature. However, even though his arguments gained immediate attention, much of it was unfavorably critical. Only in the decades following his death in 1935 did Parry's theories, especially as they were continued and expanded in the work of Albert B. Lord, win adherents.[26] It is no longer

25. Mure, *A Critical History of the Language and Literature of Ancient Greece,* 180–81.

26. Forty years after Parry's work, Sterling Dow wrote, "[T]he human brain works slowly, if at all, and there are signs that although the Parry doctrines are getting to be fairly well absorbed in England, farther away, as in Vienna, the light has not yet dawned" ("Literacy: The Palace Bureaucracies, the Dark Age, Homer," 124).

blasphemy to say that the unusual nature of the epics can be explained only if we understand the oral means of their composition.

The limited literacy of the Mycenaean Linear B appears to have disappeared in the early twelfth century with the collapse of the administrative systems that had called it forth.[27] Alphabetic literacy, introduced from the Levant, only gradually replaced complete orality from around 750 BCE. Thus, the four centuries of the Dark Age provide a rare example of a culture operating in conditions of total nonliteracy. All cultures must remember certain facts, events, and rules. In literate cultures, memory is aided by agreed-upon symbols, written "codes." In the absence of literacy, speech itself can be patterned to assist memory. "Poetized speech" is "a device contrived to produce what might be called paradoxically the oral documentation of a non-literate culture . . . a serious instrument—the only one available—for storing, preserving, and transmitting that cultural information which was felt to be important enough to require separation from the vernacular."[28]

Memory through oral tradition operates in ways markedly different from memory encoded in writing, but the difference does not exclude retention of information from the past. Fundamental to orality is the role of sound: an oral tradition is dependent on the spoken word. Because sound cannot be captured without the aid of written means or electronic technology, recall is enhanced by several means: Fixed units of speech adapted to a rhythmic meter and a focus on concrete, monumental events and subjects are essential for memorability. Another requirement is that the accounts be intelligible to their tellers and their listeners. The material remembered is selected according to the interests of society, not individual interests. Thus, traditions are societal products. When properly structured, the products have no loose ends: past and present may overlap or diverge through anachronisms or floating gaps, but the apparent discrepancies, apparent from the perspective of a literate mentality, are not troublesome to the listeners.[29]

---

27. J. A. Davison, *Companion to Homer,* 217. A. Heubeck states in "L'origine della lineare B," "[C]ontemporaneamente alla distruzione violenta della cultura micenea è andata dunque perduta anche l'arte della scritture" (Contemporary with the violent destruction of Mycenaean culture the art of writing was lost, 197). On the return of literacy, see L. Jeffery, *Archaic Greece: The City States c. 700–500 B.C.,* 25–26.

28. Eric A. Havelock, "The Transcription of the Code of a Non-literate Culture," 116.

29. Jan Vansina, *Oral Tradition as History,* 171.

That the *Iliad* and *Odyssey* originated as oral poetry is now generally accepted. As we have seen, Jason figures in the epic poems. Moreover, in our search for the historical plausibility of Jason's adventure, his presence in this body of oral poetry can be coupled with another even more recent linguistic feat, namely, the decipherment of the tablets found in Bronze Age centers on the mainland of Greece and the island of Crete. Clay tablets inscribed in the script known as Linear B have been known through excavation for approximately a century. Reading the script, however, was hampered by limited quantities of tablets and the fact that it was unattested elsewhere. Consequently, it was not until 1952 that a decipherment was announced by Michael Ventris, an architect with an amazing gift for language. Although he had circulated work notes to a number of scholars working to learn the secret of the script and had been joined in his efforts by the classicist John Chadwick, the announcement was initially greeted by more skepticism than agreement. The ongoing studies of Chadwick and an international group of scholars have vanquished the opponents' criticism of the correctness of the basic decipherment, moving preclassical Greece from the ranks of prehistoric cultures to those that are protohistoric by virtue of possessing at least limited literacy.

As a result of the decipherment, it is possible to extend a search for the voyage of the *Argo* into the Mycenaean age. In one direction of his Linear B studies, Chadwick investigated the connection between the form of Greek preserved in the tablets and that of Homeric Greek preserved by the traditional dialect. "If more than a few such words can be shown to occur on the Mycenaean tablets," he wrote, "the existence of a direct link can then be inferred."[30] His findings in 1958 were impressive, and the evidence has grown over the succeeding four decades.

The implication of this continuity is clear: the links that many archaeologists see between the Homeric epics and the Mycenaean civilization—including palaces and their locations, armor, and the use of chariots—have independent verification in similarities of language preserved in two quite different scripts. It is possible that a tale of events in the Bronze Age sung by a bard of the eighth century had its roots in the Mycenaean age. That the tale was cast in the poetized speech of oral tradition is extremely likely,

---

30. Chadwick, "Mycenaean Elements in the Homeric Dialect," 118.

for, aside from the inventories preserved in the Linear B script, there is no other evidence for the use of writing in the Greek Bronze Age.[31] The newly developed system of literacy served specific needs within Mycenaean society but was not employed for all remembrances of the culture. A fresco from the center at Pylos points to the role of orality in its depiction of a singer with "winged words" (in the form of a bird) flying from his mouth. Although changes would have occurred over time in order to render the account intelligible to listeners of later centuries, the core of the tale persisted.

The specific contents of the deciphered tablets provide more evidence about people associated with the tale. One category of words is especially tantalizing: nouns, particularly personal names, ending in -e-u (the Mycenaean form; in later Greek the form is -eus) are plentiful in the Linear B tablets. By contrast, -eus names in the classical period are extremely limited: in records from classical Attica, only 236 individuals of a total of 62,360 (that is, 0.38 percent) named people have -eus names. One conclusion, according to Anna Morpurgo Davies, has been to treat the Homeric names as purely poetic invention and to assume that Greek parents did not like poetic names. She argues, however, that this explanation is no longer possible after the decipherment of Linear B, especially in light of the fact that, in Mycenaean, there are at least 130 different -eus names out of about 1,800 names (7.26 percent).[32] She proposes an explanation based on the existence of an -e-wa suffix in Mycenaean that might have been the antecedent of the -eas suffix, which, at least in Arcadia in the classical period, replaced the -eus suffix.

In our search for an Ur-*Argonautica*, the issue of -eus names is important because they designate a good many epic heroes. Long before the decipherment of Linear B, P. Kretschmer drew attention to the patterning between two series of heroic names: earlier heroes often have names ending in -eus, whereas names of their sons are regularly common compound names.[33] For instance:

31. I have speculated on this issue in "Mycenaean Law in Its Oral Context."
32. Davies, "Personal Names and Linguistic Continuity," 35.
33. "Wie der zusammenfassende Name erst in einem etwas jüngeren Stadium der Sage eingetreten zu sein scheint" (It appears that the compound name first came into being in a somewhat earlier phase of legend) (Kretschmer, "Mythische Namen," 57).

Peleus, Achilleus	Neoptolemus
Odysseus	Telemachus
Atreus	Agamemnon, Menelaos
Neleus	Nestor
Oeneus	Meleager
Aegeus, Theseus	Hippolytus

On the list of men regularly identified as Argonauts, several have names ending in -eus: they include the Lapith Caeneus; Cepheus of Arcadia; Lynceus of Messene; Oileus, the father of Ajax; the singer Orpheus; and Peleus, the father of Achilles. The brother of Iphitus is Eurystheus of Mycenae, and Idas is the son of Aphareus of Messene. With their other companions of the sorts of Herakles, Hylas, Castor, and Polydeuces, and Jason himself, they belong to an earlier heroic generation than the heroes associated with the Trojan War. "Their adventures are not restricted by a recent tradition from the Trojan War on, but were probably originated many centuries before."[34]

Other names embedded in the Argonautic legend may appear in the Linear B texts; of particular interest are i-wa-so (PY Cn 655) (the w disappears in classical Greek, and Linear B omits final consonants; thus, Jason is a strong candidate) and ko-ki-da (KN Sd 4403) (which can be Colchidas, a version of Colchis).[35] Thus, the personal name of Iason (Jason) could be recorded in the Linear B script, and a place bearing a close resemblance to the home of the Golden Fleece may also be attested. Is it mere coincidence that most of these names occur on the tablets from Pylos, which in legend became the kingdom of Neleus after his brother, the unpleasant Pelias, had driven him from Iolkos?

In sum, the detailed analyses of personal names—onomastics—has "the potential . . . to provide hitherto and otherwise unavailable insights into ancient Greece society."[36] And, as the -eus names show, onomastics can

34. Geoffrey Kirk, Myth: Its Meaning and Functions in Ancient and Other Cultures, 177–78.
35. The inscriptions are classified by abbreviations indicating find-places (PY = Pylos, KN = Knossos), subjects (Cn = livestock, Sd = chariots and armor), and inventory numbers (655, 4403).
36. Simon Hornblower and Elaine Matthews, eds., Greek Personal Names: Their Value as Evidence, 2.

Pylos tablet CN655 with the Mycenaean Greek for i-wa-so, *possibly Jason. (Courtesy of the Department of Classics, University of Cincinnati, and Thomas Palaima)*

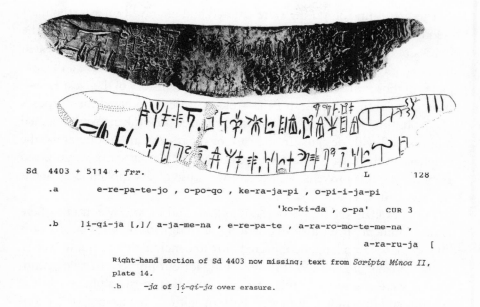

```
Sd   4403 + 5114 + frr.                                    L        128
  .a       e-re-pa-te-jo , o-po-qo , ke-ra-ja-pi , o-pi-i-ja-pi
                                    'ko-ki-da , o-pa'   CUR 3
  .b    li-qi-ja [,]/ a-ja-me-na , e-re-pa-te , a-ra-ro-mo-te-me-na ,
                                                       a-ra-ru-ja [
```

Right-hand section of Sd 4403 now missing; text from *Scripta Minoa II*,
plate 14.
.b   -*ja* of]*i-qi-ja* over erasure.

*Knossos tablet 4403 with joins from 5514 and fragments, including the Mycenaean
Greek for* ko-ki-da, *possibly* Colchis. *(With permission of Cambridge University
Press and Jean-Pierre Olivier)*

now be employed in the study of Bronze Age Greece, thanks to the decipherment of Linear B.

An Aside

I will venture to add that there is another way in which Linear B brings
us closer to people who used it: it reveals something of the very nature of
the Greek they spoke and wrote. It is, of course, impossible to re-create
the precise nature of an ancient language; even the intonation of classical
Greek is uncertain. However, the form of the Mycenaean script offers an
important clue, especially when that script is compared with scripts employed in earlier and contemporary cultures.[37]

37. An interesting comparative study is J. Bottéro, C. Herrenschmidt, and J.-P. Vernant,
Ancestor of the West: Writing, Reasoning, and Religion in Mesopotamia, Elam, and Greece.

The first forms of writing were painted and engraved images: the marvelous cave paintings of southern France and Spain, carvings like the phases of the moon on pieces of bone, and designs on clay vessels. Such images convey meaning as well as pleasure, but they do not reveal the language of those who created them. Later in the prehistory of the Near East—from the eighth millennium BCE—tokens were introduced for purposes of accounting. Many were unmarked, but over time tokens were notched and marked with designs. In the case of the tokens in Mesopotamia, the language of their users is known because the Sumerian script was derived from the complex tokens. However, the nature of the spoken language is not revealed.

In the Bronze Age scripts of Mesopotamia and Egypt, by contrast, there is development "from a simple writing of things to the writing of words and sounds . . . no longer connected only to concrete things, but to words, to the spoken language."[38] It is interesting for our purpose that vowel notations were absent. And this absence continued in the alphabets of the second- and first-millennium Near Eastern cultures that have signs for consonants but not for vowels. Although weak consonants can be used to indicate the nature of the vowel—for instance, Hebrew *yod* indicates vowel i and *e*—it is the consonantal root that carries the meaning of the sign.

Linear B departed from this practice (as did Linear Elamite): its eighty-seven signs constitute a syllabary in which signs denote five vowels, standing alone as a single syllable, and each of twelve consonants combine with each of the vowels.[39] Such syllabic writing "reproduces the sounds that are heard by the listener, notes the sounds that strike the eardrum and penetrate within the subject."[40] In short, it comes close to the sound of the language itself. Now, familiarity with the Greek language of any period discloses a great fondness for vowels. From Homeric Greek to classical to modern, vowel sounds are abundant—to the distress of many who cower in the face of reading Greek words, even in transliterated form. This same fondness reaches back to Greek speakers of the second millennium.

Sound, or sonority, determined spelling conventions, as complex lin-

38. J. Bottéro, "Religion and Reasoning in Mesopotamia," in ibid., 24.

39. Other signs were special variants of these vowels and consonants; for example, a second sign for vowel *a* indicates the association of the *a* vowel with a "glide" sound, *a + j*.

40. C. Herrenschmidt, "Writing between Visible and Invisible Worlds in Iran, Israel, and Greece," in Bottéro, Herrenschmidt, and Vernant, *Ancester of the West*, 82.

guistic analysis has determined. Roger Woodward has examined the seemingly arcane rules of Linear B that regularly omit certain consonantal sounds: a final consonant is regularly not indicated, and in combinations of vowel + consonant and consonant + vowel + consonant, the final consonant is usually ignored. When consonant clusters are written, their forms are based on the orthographic strength of consonants; the ranking from high to low strength moves from stops (k, p, q, t), to fricatives (s, z), to nasals (n, m), to glides (w, j), with liquids of least strength (r, l). Those consonants that *are* indicated are given a vowel on the basis of their place in this hierarchy. Vowels are added; they are of greater sonority than consonants, which are sometimes expendable. Woodward suggests that we should not be surprised that a scribe of the second millennium BCE "should possess sufficient linguistic sophistication and insight to perceive that language sounds fall into natural classes and that these classes differ in relative sonority. Ancient humanity was no less observant and ingenious than its modern counterpart."[41]

Adding philology and linguistics to our complement of tools enriches the results of archaeography by adding names of places and people to the physical evidence as well as suggesting their very speech. This composite picture can be given fuller detail by turning to some of the scientific contributions that have been incorporated into archaeology during the past fifty years.

Science as Partner

Even with possible places and people—and perhaps the sound of their speech—the voyage of the Argonauts has regularly presented a real obstacle to the search for a Mycenaean origin. Although Bronze Age Greeks seem to have been competent sailors, entering the Black Sea is difficult even today. How could a Bronze Age boat survive the narrow entrance of the Bosporus?

The current in the Bosporus is on average about three knots, but north-

41. Woodward, *Greek Writing from Knossos to Homer: A Linguistic Interpretation of the Origin of the Greek Alphabet and the Continuity of Ancient Greek Literacy*, 246–47. Woodward states, "If the first of two successive consonants occupies a position on the hierarchy which is higher than or equal to that of the second, then it will be written with a [consonant-vowel] symbol whose vocalic component is identical to the vowel which follows the cluster; otherwise it will be written with the CV symbol whose vocalic component is identical to the vowel which precedes the cluster" (72).

eastern winds often double its speed in the summer, which is the regular sailing season in the Aegean. Since these winds blow contrary to a ship trying to enter the Black Sea, they make passage extremely difficult. In 1948, Rhys Carpenter demonstrated the need for a fast-rowing ship, the penteconter, to prevail against the winds blowing against a ship trying to traverse the Bosporus and thereby gain access to the Black Sea. The usual view is that Greeks gained such a ship only in the Archaic Age, that is, the seventh and sixth centuries BCE. Consequently, if one persisted in seeking an Ur-*Argonautica* deriving from the Bronze Age, a solution was to conclude that an earlier tale was located in more manageable waters and was relocated to the Black Sea in later times. Fritz Graf concludes that "localizing of the land of the Colchians in the southeastern corner of the Black Sea cannot be very old," that is, "a fundamental change was made in the story during the archaic period."[42]

Carpenter's findings have been questioned on the basis of more precise knowledge of natural forces such as currents and winds. Articles by Benjamin Labaree and A. J. Graham in 1957 and 1958, respectively, provided fuller information on the Bosporus conditions than Carpenter's article had included.[43] The *Black Sea Pilot,* a maritime guide for the area, reveals that although northeastern winds do make sailing through the Bosporus extremely difficult, there are times when a high-pressure area lies over the Black Sea, depressing its level and creating southerly winds in the Aegean. Thus, although passage into the Black Sea is virtually impossible for twelve days in the average sailing month, about ten days have southwestern winds that check the current and actually serve as favorable following winds.[44] At these times a vessel could complete the passage in eight to nine hours under sail alone.

Drawing also upon ethnography, Graham notes other aids to sailors. Countercurrents or back eddies flowing northward up the sides of the bay are used by all ships today; by lowering an anchor into the countercurrent, the boat is dragged along by its force. Small boats are often towed from the land. Quoting a second-century CE source, Graham paints a

---

42. Carpenter, "The Greek Penetration of the Black Sea"; Graf, "Medea, the Enchantress from Afar: Remarks on a Well-Known Myth," 32.

43. See Labaree, "How the Greeks Sailed into the Black Sea"; and Graham, "The Date of the Greek Penetration of the Black Sea."

44. I am grateful to Robert Carter for this information.

vivid picture of the ingenuity of hard-pressed sailors: "[S]ometimes when the current slackens a little they struggle against the stream at the very edge of the landing place, just by the rocks, using the rocks as supports for their oars and strengthening their power on sea by help from the land." Furthermore, Graham believes:

> In the areas of Greek navigation there is no place more suited to give rise to the myth of the moving or clashing rocks than the Bosporus. Ancient geographers were right to point out in explanation of the myth that the strait seems closed from afar, and as you come nearer and move from one side to the other, it seems to open and close. When one adds to the appearance the formidable current, one sees that the Bosporus provides a very suggestive factual basis for the *Symplegades* myth. And if the myth arose from the passage of the Bosporus, then the *Odyssey's* reference to it, however vague, shows that Greek sailors had penetrated into the Black Sea before the *Odyssey* was composed.[45]

Moreover, a new explanation of the penteconter's history dates its origin to the thirteenth century BCE, that is, the Mycenaean age. Michael Wedde makes a compelling case in his study of the nature of Bronze Age ships based on the evidence of representations, or iconography.[46] Evidence exists from the late Bronze Age for partial decking to create hulls capable of carrying the greater weight of a second level of rowers. Two advantages of the decking are especially pertinent to our present pursuit: first, the vessel would be capable of greater speed, and, second, the greater weight produced by adding a second level would provide greater rigidity, making the hull more resistant to impact. In addition to decking, developments in sails and their rigging occurred at approximately the same time. A loose-footed sail that appears to be an Aegean invention brought greater scope for trimming the sail to suit wind conditions. And, as we have seen, wind conditions were a major impediment to sailing the Bosporus.

45. On aids to sailors, see Graham, "Date of Greek Penetration," 30–31, which follows an account by Dionysius Byzantius, *Anaplus Borpori,* dating probably to the second century CE and, thus, offers evidence from antiquity. On the clashing rocks, see ibid., 38.

46. See Wedde, *Towards a Hermeneutics of Aegean Bronze Age Ship Imagery.*

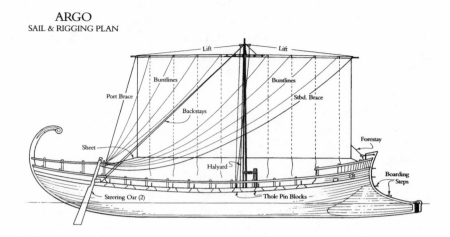

Sail and rigging plan of the modern Argo. *(Courtesy the Severin Archive)*

Another kind of evidence takes the form of a fairly recent feat directed by Timothy Severin who challenged the opinion that no Bronze Age ship could have made the voyage into the Black Sea. His challenge took the form of building a fifty-four-foot-long galley constructed over three years using Bronze Age techniques. It carried a three-hundred-square-foot sail on a twenty-four-foot mast and was equipped with twenty oars. Named the *Argo,* the vessel set out from Greece—Volos, of course—on May 3, 1984, on an intended fifteen-hundred-mile journey to the eastern coast of the Black Sea.

The story is told in a book, *The Jason Voyage,* and on a video produced by Films for the Humanities. Crossing the Aegean and sweeping through the Dardanelles offered little challenge. The eighteen miles of six- to seven-knot current through the Bosporus was quite a different matter. When the current hit the vessel, swinging her bow, "Argo hung, posed like a salmon fighting rapids. We barely advanced." Yet they did enter the Black Sea, finding it deserving of its name, "axenos," or "inhospitable." For two days and nights the *Argo* with its crew was driven out to sea. Like a Bronze Age ship it had no compass, making it difficult to take bearings, especially when the heavens were obscured by clouds. In fact, Turkish papers reported that the *Argo* and all hands had been lost at sea. Somehow,

The modern Argo *at sea. (Courtesy the Severin Archive)*

in spite of fog, on the third day they found themselves back on course within striking distance of their goal, "Georgia," where they received a hero's welcome. During their stay on land, more pieces of evidence came to light. Severin, quoted in a *National Geographic* article, claimed justifiably that "our Argo showed that the voyage could be made."[47] And a rather

47. Severin, "Jason's Voyage: In Search of the Golden Fleece," 415, 416, 420.

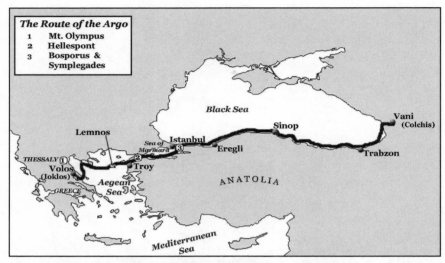

The route of the Argo. *(Electronically drawn by Lance Jenott)*

unusual form of ethnology produced a welcome insight at its place of destination: Severin and his modern Argonauts learned that sheepskins pegged on boards are sunk in streambeds to trap gold carried in the streams from the Ural Mountains.

Considered together, the ability to negotiate Poseidon's realm from the Neolithic age, the presence of an early form of the penteconter in the Mycenaean age, and new understanding of conditions in the Bosporus strait strengthen a case that Aegean goods found in the Black Sea littoral may have been carried by Mycenaean ships. But are there grounds for connecting this skill with a voyage akin to that remembered in Apollonius's epic?

What Is Myth?

It is time to return to our point of departure: the identification of the story of Jason as a myth, that category in which "little distinction [was] made between the real and the unreal," and the imagination "was vividly alive and not checked by reason."[48] This sort of definition associates myth with fairy tale and fiction. Other more sensitive explanations have gained favor.

48. E. Hamilton, *Mythology,* 13.

Martin P. Nilsson was preternaturally insightful in drawing out the implications of the emerging evidence of the first civilization of Greece by linking the material evidence with myth and legend. In his *Mycenaean Origin of Greek Mythology,* published more than seventy years ago, he argues for the heuristic value of myths, reminding readers that mythology had served well as a guide to the first discoveries of the heroic age. Heinrich Schliemann, with Homer in hand as a guide to locations of Troy and Mycenae, is an excellent case in point. Moreover, Nilsson argues that a thorough comparison of the sites to which the myth cycles are attached with sites where finds from the Mycenaean age have been made shows a close correspondence. Agamemnon, leader of the Greek host at Troy, was king of Mycenae; Herakles is linked with Tiryns; the Oedipus cycle is centered on Thebes; Theseus is from Athens; garrulous Nestor rules from Pylos. Each of these locations has revealed a citadel dating to the late Bronze Age. Certain of these places also had a later history. Thebes was one of the major poleis of classical Greece. However, most of the centers of myth cycles were either absent or insignificant in the classical age, though they were extremely impressive in the Mycenaean era. Mycenae, the mighty citadel of Agamemnon, could field eighty hoplites against the Persian invasion. On these grounds, Nilsson concludes that the mythic cycles in their chief outlines go back to the Mycenaean age.[49]

Iolkos fits this pattern neatly. It dates to the Bronze Age, although there is evidence of continuity into the Iron Age. But what was Iolkos in the classical age beyond a memory of a heroic past? The main power in the Gulf of Pagasai was now Pagasai. Thus, the legend of the Argonauts, like that of the Achaean coalition led by Agamemnon, accords with the Bronze Age but is poorly suited to conditions of the classical period.

Nilsson's conclusions on the nature of myth rest on the stunning archaeological findings of the late nineteenth and early twentieth centuries. Far more disciplines have been joined in efforts to understand the true function of myth. From exploration of the unconscious, linked with the name of Freud, to Jung's explanation of the universal symbolism of all myths and Lévi-Strauss's embedded structuralism, the study of myth has become something of a discipline in its own right. In his Sather Lecture of 1969, Geoffrey Kirk made a number of observations that are particularly

49. Nilsson, *Mycenaean Origin,* 28.

useful for our understanding of the Greek age of heroes and its remembrance. A useful beginning is his realization that "we can see the differences between legend and myth undisturbed by any terminological confusion, since Greek, far from having too many words for different kinds of tale, has too few." The surviving great legend the *Iliad* "is obviously historicizing in content." Kirk is not alone in believing that some kind of memory of the past provides the foundation for a tale that mixes legend, saga, and folklore with what, in other cultures, is termed myth. Most scholars acknowledge that the Homeric epics assumed their final form in the late Dark Age or early archaic period. Therefore, such a definition of these categories of tradition based on the Homeric epics may have little relation to myths and legends of the Mycenaean age not only because of their distance in time but also because they were of a period in which some have maintained that humans had not yet developed full consciousness. Kirk offers sound thoughts on the view that an age of reason dawned suddenly for Greeks only in the Archaic Age, concluding, "What we see in Hesiod—that mixture of personification, allegory, speculative myth, fable, literal statement, loose association, intermittent logic, and native shrewdness—was probably around in Greece for a very long time before him; and the stage when virtually all theorizing unconsciously took narrative and purely mythical form may have lain thousands of years in the past."[50]

It is important to bear in mind the continued reliance on oral transmission, even when the Linear B script was developed for its restricted uses. Most peoples have stories, even groups without literacy. Information worth remembering can be encoded in poetized language that serves as a tool for recall. Kirk's conjecture that "mythology had provided a conceptual language, long before Hesiod, for some sort of systematic discussion about, and ordering of, society and the outside world" is valuable for concluding our search for an Ur-*Argonautica*.[51] We began with a "myth" originally seen as a fictitious story, but perhaps we will end with a "myth" defined as a means to preserve memory of past reality.

50. Kirk, *Myth*, 32, 241. Julian Jaynes argues in *The Origin of Consciousness in the Breakdown of the Bicameral Mind* that he sees "outcroppings of something close to subjective consciousness in the *Iliad*" (73).
51. Kirk, *Myth*, 247.

A Mycenaean *Argonautica*?

The work of Moses I. Finley was a fundamental turning point in many areas of our understanding of early Greece, among them our attitudes toward oral traditions. Finley argues that the myths and legends upon which the Homeric epics are based supply "the materials for the study of a real world of real men, a world of history and not of fiction." Marcel Detienne has reached a similar conclusion in his examination of the differences between accounts preserved orally and those committed to writing, namely, that, lacking other documents "which would make it possible to establish the 'reality' of the history being sought after, consistency is the only guarantee of authenticity."[52] Let us examine the clues that exist for a Bronze Age *Argonautica* for signs of consistency.

Archaeological excavation has uncovered a site with Mycenaean remains in the Gulf of Pagasai, the region where (mythical) Iolkos was traditionally located. Comparison with Mycenaean centers excavated earlier suggests that it was the northernmost citadel-centered kingdom in the late Bronze Age configuration of Greek society. Recent investigation has produced even more indications of the ancient vitality of the area near Iolkos in the finds at neighboring Dimini. Survey archaeology demonstrates that the land in the region was valuable for agricultural production and animal husbandry and that the region overlooks a bay with a good harbor, still important today. Through specific artifactual evidence we can narrow our time frame to approximately three hundred years—around 1500–1200 BCE. It is true that Thessaly continued to be prominent in the classical and Hellenistic periods, but in the classical period Iolkos itself was unimportant. Moreover, a tie between the *Argonautica* and Iolkos nicely suits Nilsson's thesis that myth cycles are linked to major Mycenaean sites.

Later written evidence reveals that Jason and his adventures were known to bards of the late Dark Age: The *Argo* was "widely-sung," according to Homer. That the oral tradition of the bards reaches back to Mycenaean times is indicated by linguistic similarities between the Greek of Linear B and that of the Homeric poems. What is more, it is the nature of oral tradition in a culture without literacy to be "conservative"; it is the

---

52. Finley, *The World of Odysseus*, 49; Detienne, *The Creation of Mythology*, 25.

means, through poetized language, to recall important information from one generation to the next. Being poetized, the language may bear closer resemblance to myth, legend, or folktale than to history, blurring distinctions between those "categories."

Mycenaean goods may have been carried in the ships of other peoples. On the other hand, nautical evidence suggests that the kind of ship necessary to move through the treacherous waters of the Bosporus was at hand in the second millennium in the essential form of the penteconter. Furthermore, recreation of navigational skills in a galley constructed in accord with Bronze Age technology demonstrated that wind and the strength of twenty oarsmen could carry this 1980s *Argo* from Volos to the eastern end of the Black Sea.

Finally, dating of the varied evidence by more precise means tends to converge on an earlier part of the Mycenaean age. Iolkos was an important site during the late Bronze Age, with two successive large buildings. Troy VI, perhaps the port of call for eastward travel by sea, flourished from about 1700 to 1250–1230. Mycenaean finds in the Black Sea include a number from the earlier part of the period. The Argonauts' names reflect a generation earlier than that of the Trojan War heroes.

Altogether, a fair degree of convergence emerges from the several categories of information. Without doubt, more evidence is forthcoming.

- Ongoing archaeological work at Iolkos-Dimini will surely enhance our knowledge of that site.

- Human bones are evidence of physical appearance—height, shape of head—and if enough bones from the head are preserved, it is possible to reconstruct the facial likeness. The technique has been used to give images of other Mycenaeans.[53] Along with human bones, a tooth or two might be uncovered to provide material for DNA testing.

- Inasmuch as Linear B tablets derive from the major centers, written information may join the physical evidence. The tablets from Thebes have come to light far more recently than those from Pylos, Knossos, and Mycenae. How rewarding it would be

53. As has been done by J. H. Musgrave et al. in "Seven Faces from Grave Circle B at Mycenae."

to find *i-wa-so* at Iolkos as well as at Pylos. And should tablets be discovered, they would provide additional evidence of the physical nature of their makers. Akin to other clay objects, the tablets bear fingerprints and palm prints, the latter from the work of flattening lumps of clay into the desired shapes. Each finger and each palm are unique, and, consequently, these prints identify individuals in antiquity just as they do in modern times.[54] An examination of the palm prints on the tablets can reveal the number of individuals engaged in shaping the clay. Coupling these findings with the results of styles of writing on the tablets can offer insights into questions such as: What was the ratio of tablet makers to scribes? Did people work in groups or teams? In other words, we can insert people into the picture of Mycenaean records.

• Archaeological investigation in the Black Sea is gaining momentum; thus, the quantity of evidence for a Mycenaean connection may grow absolutely and also link Mycenaean objects to particular sites in the Black Sea, even the kingdom of Aietes at Colchis, which has yet to be found.

• Comparison between these objects and objects produced at individual mainland Greek centers would help identify the particular communities involved in the trade since spectroscopic analysis of clay from vessels can pinpoint the source of the clay.

Our image of Jason at present derives from the *Argonautica* of Apollonius. As Peter Levi concludes, rather unkindly quoting Michael Bentley, "It is a pretty poem, Mr. Apollonius, but it is not Homer." Nor it is Mycenaean. More helpfully, Peter Green places our *Argonautica* in its context of the third century; it shows its "cultural burden" even while it is held together by an old traditional legend.[55] Nonetheless, by drawing upon the multiple disciplines at our disposal in the belief that they convey concrete information and are not without fixed meaning, there are sufficient clues to carry the account back into the "heroic age," thereby inserting people and their activities into the story of the first civilization of Greece.

54. See K. E. Sjöquist and Paul Åstrom, *Pylos: Palmprints and Palmleaves*.
55. Levi, *The Pelican History of Greek Literature*, 421; Green, *Alexander to Actium*, 208.

こ濫

The Birth of the Author

Greek history reaches back to the Bronze Age, yet its path from the second millennium into the first was not direct. Massive disturbances throughout the entire eastern Mediterranean disrupted the civilizations of Egypt and the Near East while, at the same time, they buckled contemporary civilizations of the Aegean region and Anatolia. In Greece, the protohistorical culture of the Mycenaeans would not be resuscitated. Rather, four centuries of slow transformation of the remnants of the Mycenaean way of life were leavened by monumental difficulties of simple survival in a time remembered as the Dark Age. The struggle was worth the effort: the final product was the classical or golden age of Greece.

In spite of the massive troubles, important continuity linked the phases of Greek life: the language for one, people for another, and a sustenance pattern rooted in the land. Gone, however, were the citadel centers with their hierarchical, administrative structures and international ties. Missing as well was the syllabic script of Linear B. In its place, by the mid-eighth century, was an alphabetic script of (eventually) twenty-four signs. The introduction of alphabetic writing, according to Eric Havelock, one of its ardent admirers, "was to alter the character of human culture. . . . The Greeks did not just invent an alphabet; they invented literacy and the literate basis of modern thought."[1] Its advent is also appreciated by historians as the tool needed to pursue the study of history.

Greek scholars are fortunate to have access to two of the first products of that revolution in the form of poems attributed to the poet-farmer

1. Havelock, "The Greek Alphabet," 82.

Drawing of late classical mosaic of Hesiod by Monnus. (Drawn by Anne Lou Robkin and reprinted with her permission)

Hesiod. Examination of the relationship between the Homeric epics and the poems of Hesiod gives a date of around 700–670 for the Hesiodic works. Although the earliest surviving samples of alphabetic writing are brief inscriptions scratched on pottery or added to statues, the poetic form of Hesiod's works is evidence of sustained composition: the shorter poem consists of 828 lines, the longer of 1,022. The quality of the poems has not been uniformly praised, yet even criticism of their poetic merit is revealing of the author's purpose. As an editor of one of the poems observed, "The author began to write a series of admonitions, and such was his enthusiasm for his subject that he almost succeeded in writing a fine poem. That he did not quite succeed in a task which he had never really set himself must not be counted a great fault."[2] Surprising as it may sound, such criticism is valuable in appreciating the nature of Hesiod's poems. They are didactic in intent: a farmer's manual, *Works and Days* describes the benefits of hard work and the means of proper management of a farm, and *Theogony*

2. On dating, see Richard Janko, *Homer, Hesiod, and the Hymns: Diachronic Development in Epic Diction,* 200; on the quality of poetry, see T. A. Sinclair, *Hesiod: Works and Days,* xi.

recounts the history of the universe traced through the genealogy of the gods. The heroic age of the *Iliad* and *Odyssey* has been left behind.

Many other differences besides subject separate the Homeric epics from Hesiod's didactic poems. The openly didactic intent of *Works and Days* and the careful ordering of divine genealogy in *Theogony* deviate from the embedded revelation of values and order of the *Iliad* and *Odyssey*. Hesiod himself asserts the basis of a good life, whereas Homer rarely intrudes into his poetry. And the farmer-poet enters his poems directly, reminding us, "The Muses once taught Hesiod to sing sweet songs, / while he was shepherding his lambs" (*Theogony*, lines 215–16).

In sum, historians may have a window in these poems into the time and life of a particular person, a window with a clearer focus than the evidence available for identifying Jason in the late Bronze Age. In that search we were able to suggest the physical and material world of a person living in the Mycenaean age, as well as to identify activities that sustained life and the horizons that the world encompassed. Although we can re-create the language that a Jason spoke and imagine his appearance, we have no way of learning his thoughts, motives, emotions, or values. With Hesiod's poems, on the other hand, a named person offers an account of, and his feelings about, his own time.

Or so it would seem, for the crisis in the human-centered disciplines has complicated such a straightforward approach. As the evidence in this case is largely textual, postmodern relativism has undermined the view that a single known individual can be identified as the author of *Theogony* and *Works and Days*. As a result of the process of deconstruction, some believe that "Hesiod" is a fictitious construct of every-poet who sang or wrote didactic poetry akin to *Works and Days* and *Theogony*.[3] The three main bases of this conclusion are the question of authorship in products that took shape in a nonliterate society, prominence of stock elements and figures, and an inclination to deconstruct not only the text but also the societal backdrop of the text. A primary concern of this search then will be to ask whether these issues preclude an understanding of a man living in the early seventh century BCE. Ruth Scodel, for example, wonders why

3. This is the conclusion of Robert Lamberton in his *Hesiod,* who dismisses not only the person Hesiod but all of the biographical information embedded in the poems.

we must make Hesiod a postmodernist.[4] To verify the possible existence of Hesiod, both philology and oral tradition must be used. The manner in which he was viewed by later Greeks will also be of service, as will the picture that emerges from the poems themselves.

In addition, to determine the validity of using Hesiod's poetry to understand the person and his world requires many of the same tools used in a search for Jason. Archaeological evidence will be needed to determine whether the world described in the poems bears any resemblance to Greece in the late eighth and early seventh centuries. Since Hesiod describes his own home in a place he calls Askra, we must also consider topography and the survival of named locations into later times. However, because the poems provide our primary evidence for the life and views of the person, they will be our beginning, as the Muses were the beginning for Hesiod.

The Poems

Works and Days and *Theogony* belong to a larger body of poetry grouped under the designation the Boeotian School. That term serves both to distinguish this poetry from the Ionian verse linked to Homer and to assign authorship to Hesiod. Until the Hellenistic age, the entire body of the Boeotian School was credited to Hesiod. Critical study by Alexandrian scholars demonstrated that the items usually included under the name were the work neither of a single person nor of a single period. Of the fourteen longer works, *Works and Days* and *Theogony* are, by general—although not unanimous—consensus, attributed to Hesiod.[5]

The preface of *Theogony* (lines 1–115) offers important information about the poet, even his name: "Now [the muses] taught Hesiod lovely song" (22). The remaining 907 lines rehearse the genealogy of the gods, and the author seldom enters the account. Beginning with Chaos, the poem next turns attention to Earth, then tells of the generations of "the deathless ones

---

4. Scodel, "Poetic Authority and Oral Tradition in Hesiod and Pindar," 113.

5. The *Catalogue of Famous Women,* of which a number of fragments remain, is perhaps the strongest other candidate for Hesiodic authorship. In his treatment of ancient Greek literature, Peter Levi—a classicist and poet—argues against this identification, stating firmly, "I do not believe it could possibly be by Hesiod." Its value is "as a collection of mythology" (*Pelican History,* 56).

who hold the peaks of snowy Olympus" (188), and concludes with the present divine generation under the sway of Zeus. *Theogony* belongs to the types of accounts that are typical of oral traditions: personal family traditions, group accounts of information important to an entire society, and traditions of origin and genesis. Genealogical reckoning is the usual form of these accounts.[6]

Works and Days is more autobiographical than *Theogony:* when he gives advice, Hesiod speaks in the first person. And giving advice is the main purpose of this example of wisdom literature, a genre that has deep roots in the ancient Mediterranean world. After calling upon the Muses in a short preface, the author announces that "I should like to tell true things" (11). Those truths begin with stories, homilies, and myths giving insight to one Perses—we discover later that he is the author's brother—and to the lords, who we learn are "gift devourers." The first story describes the two kinds of strife (Eris), one bad in fostering war and quarrels, the other good in pushing men to compete with others in hard work, as when potter strives with potter, craftsman with craftsman, minstrel with minstrel, and even beggar with beggar (25–26). Perses is urged to avoid the first and follow the second. The next story explains why this condition exists by recounting the myth of Prometheus's theft of fire, which greatly angered Zeus. His retaliation took the form of directing the creation of Pandora, a sweet and lovely maid with a face like that of an immortal goddess but who became a plague to man by loosening the lid of the great storage pot that contained a myriad of plagues for mortals.

Conditions were not always so unhappy, the poem explains through the account of the Ages of Man. From a golden age when mortals lived like the gods, without sorrow and free from grief and toil, life worsened through the ages of silver and bronze and the time of the heroes to the present Iron Age, when men never rest from labor and sorrow by day and perishing at night. The final tale seems to reflect that unhappy condition in an animal fable recounting the plight of the nightingale carried off in the talons of a hawk. "The lords will understand this fable," the poet concludes before advising Perses to avoid violence and adhere to that which is just. "Zeus is watching, yes even you my lords, with his three myriads of deathless watchers. So make straight rather than crooked judgments." Since both

6. See Vansina, "Oral Tradition as Process," in *Oral Tradition as History.*

gods and men are angered by lazy folk, it is man's lot to work in order to provide for himself and his family. But gaining wealth by evil means is worse than poverty (paraphrase of lines 248–319).

With this injunction, the poem turns to a description of the proper way to work and to provide a livelihood (383–617), followed by instruction should Perses be determined to travel by sea to profit from trade (618–94). Then the poem offers advice on proper behavior to avoid angering the gods (695–764). Finally, the account turns to describe the merits and demerits of particular days as, for example, the thirteenth day of the waxing month, which is bad for sowing but the best day for putting in plants (765–828). Some find this to be a "free-wheeling section," whereas others are more generous in believing that "the Days forms the logical end point: we began with Ages, moved to the calendar year and now end with the month. Within the month we move from days to parts of days."[7]

The poems bear the characteristics of oral composition, and classical Greeks coupled Hesiod with Homer. In his *Histories*, Herodotus claimed on the authority of the priestesses of Zeus's sanctuary and oracle at Dodona that Homer and Hesiod lived no more than four hundred years before his own time, that is, the mid-fifth century. A "curious work" dating back to roughly 400 BCE recounts a contest between Homer and Hesiod in which the Hellenes applauded Homer for his extraordinary verses, yet the king awarded the prize tripod to Hesiod, "declaring that it was right that he who called upon men to follow peace and husbandry should have the prize rather than one who dwelt on war and slaughter." Modern scholars make the comparison by means of the presence of signs of oral composition in both poets.[8]

It is now commonly accepted that the poems ascribed to Hesiod and to Homer are the products of a long oral tradition. The limited literacy of the Mycenaean Linear B script appears to have disappeared in the early twelfth

7. M. L. West, *Hesiod: Works and Days*, 326; Richard Hamilton, *The Architecture of Hesiod's Poetry*, 84.

8. Hugh G. Evelyn-White, trans., *Hesiod: The Homeric Hymns and Homerica*, 587. The signs of truly oral composition include a highly complex system of formulas, the observance of the principle of economy, naturalness of formular extension and articulation, and traditional details of rhythm and enjambment. As G. P. Edwards concludes, "In general [Hesiod] appears to stand in substantially the same position as Homer" (*The Language of Hesiod in Its Traditional Context*, 190).

century with the collapse of the administrative systems that had called it forth.[9] Consequently, the four centuries of the Dark Age provide a rare example of a culture operating in conditions of total nonliteracy when essential information as well as stories and songs were rendered memorable by poetized speech shaped by blocks of words, known as formulas, adapted to a fixed poetic meter. These formulas aid memory in being easily understood and pleasing to the ear. Thus, they are durable over decades and even centuries, with modifications necessary to preserve both intelligibility and pleasure. Such durability involves multiple singers performing traditional tales over long periods of time.

Those oral traditions that were most enduring or valued or both were captured in a more permanent form with the return of literacy in the eighth century. Four of the earliest products of this process are the *Iliad*, *Odyssey*, *Theogony*, and *Works and Days*, listed here in the order produced by Richard Janko's examination of the traditional and innovative elements within the traditional diction of epic:

Iliad	750–725
Odyssey	743–713
Theogony	700–665
Works and Days	690–650

He adopts dates in the middle of these ranges for his composite figure of the development of the epic tradition.[10]

People and Places

To locate Hesiod in time and place requires the correspondence of various kinds of evidence that we sought in searching for an Ur-*Argonautica*.

---

9. The work of Milman Parry was the turning point for our understanding of the language of Greek oral poetry. His papers were collected by his son (Adam Parry, ed., *The Making of Homeric Verse: The Collected Papers of Milman Parry*). On the disappearance of writing, see Davison, *Companion to Homer*, 217; and Heubeck, "L'origine della lineare B," 197.

10. Janko, *Homer, Hesiod, and the Hymns*, 200. The conclusions have found considerable favor. David Tandy notes that only one person is "unforgivingly critical" (*Warriors into Traders*, 14).

One category is names of other people and places that are identified by more than a reference in the poems attached to the name Hesiod. Specific names of people and places are embedded in both poems. Can they be corroborated by other sources?

Both poems have a *prooemium,* or preface. *Theogony* begins with an invocation to the Helikonian Muses who dance on the great sacred mountain of Helikon in Boeotia. There they wash their bodies in the spring of Hippokrene and the streams of Permessos and Olmeios (lines 1–7). The preface then discloses that these Muses with sweet voices taught Hesiod lovely song while he was pasturing sheep below the sacred mountain named Helikon (22–23), telling him, "We know how to speak many falsehoods as if they were true, / but we also know, when we wish, to sing of true things" (27–28). The shorter *prooemium* of *Works and Days,* a mere nine lines, also invokes the Muses but adds a plea to their father Zeus, "Come! See and hear me!" (9). The speaker does not identify himself at this point, although in the final line of the preface he addresses Perses, identified in line 37 as his brother. Later in the poem (650–60), when describing his single voyage by sea, he claims to have won an eared tripod for his victory in song, which he offered to the Helikonian Muses, his teachers. The match between the role of the Helikonian Muses in the two poems is encouraging inasmuch as the poet does not identify himself directly in *Works and Days.* Corroboration is also at hand in a fragment of the lyric poet Bacchylides (ca. 520–450), who quoted the words "Whomsoever the immortals honor, the good report of mortals also follows him" as those of Hesiod, "servant of the sweet Muses."[11]

The body of *Works and Days* expands on the elements of the prefaces and adds information of other kinds. The poet addresses that poem to a brother, Perses, whom he constantly charges to work to avoid famine (299). Work is not disgrace, but idleness is (311); work and then work even harder, he admonishes (381). In addition to being lazy, Perses is inclined to think about trade by sea, which the poet thinks a witless notion. Thus, he warns his brother on this matter, too: both land and sea are filled with evils (101). A father to both the poet and his brother is described: in need of a secure livelihood, their father left his home in northern Asia Minor, in

11. Evelyn-White, *Hesiod,* 280, 281.

the town of Kyme, and eventually came to "this place," namely, Askra (633–35). He is not named, but tradition has assigned the name Dios to him. Other pieces of family history can be inferred; a mother named Pyki-mede,[12] and perhaps a son of the poet who cries out, "Now may I myself not be righteous / nor my son, since it is hard to be a righteous man / if the more unjust man has the greater right" (270–72). It is worth noting at the outset that the names Perses and Dios are not "invented." They are attested in other written evidence from central Greece: Perses from Thebes around 300 BCE and Dios from Thebes in the third or second century BCE and from Megara in the fourth century.[13]

Particular places are also named in the poems: Askra, Kyme, Thebes, Aulis, Chalkis, Mount Helikon with its springs and streams, and Mount Olympus. Askra and Kyme are named together in the account of the father of the poet and Perses:

> Then he came to this place, crossing the wide sea,
> having left Aeolian Kyme, in a black ship.
>
> . . . .
>
> He settled close to Helikon in this wretched hamlet,
> Askra, bad in winter, difficult in summer, never good.
> (635–36, 639–40)

Archaeology joins with written evidence to demonstrate the existence of both settlements. Kyme was one of the early settlements on the north-western coast of Asia Minor. Its founders are identified as Cleues and Malaos, reputed to be grandsons of Agamemnon. Later local historians as-signed a date of 1120 BCE for the foundation, a period that also accords with archaeological evidence: pottery discovered at the site includes eleventh-century protogeometric ware and continues with examples of

---

12. *The Contest of Homer and Hesiod* 317–18.

13. P. M. Frazer and E. Matthews, eds., *Lexicon of Greek Personal Names*, vol. 1, *Aegean Islands, Cyprus, Cyrenaica*; vol. 2, *Attica*; vol. 3A, *The Peloponnese, Western Greece, Sicily, and Magna Graecia*; vol. 3B, *Central Greece from the Megarid to Thessaly*. Dios is a common name appearing in a number of regions: Delos, Chalkis, Eretria, Ios, Kos, Paros, Rhodes, Thasos, Athens, Poros, Tegea in Arkadia, and in southern Italy and Katana in Sicily. The name Hes-iod is attested at Eretria, Thasos, Athens, and Megalopolis in Arkadia. A Perses is named from Andros, Athens, Kerkyra, and Syracuse.

Corinthian late-geometric and early-proto-Corinthian style into the styles prevalent in the early classical period of the seventh century and later.[14] Initial settlement at the traditional date would have followed on the difficulties of the late twelfth and eleventh centuries, a period when lingering post-Mycenaean sites on the mainland of Greece declined and even disappeared, leaving a puzzling picture of vanishing people. Disappearance is not explained by increased burials during this period, but it can be understood in light of dispersal to other areas of the Aegean and eastern Mediterranean.

Of the eventual twelve cities of this Aeolian part of Asia Minor, Kyme was one of the most successful, being favored with fertile soil and an ample port. Herodotus describes the soil as better than that of the Ionian region of Asia Minor (1.149) and reports that it was in the harbor of Kyme that Xerxes wintered his fleet after retreating from Greece in 480 (8.130). That harbor was important in earlier times as well. Fragments of the writings of fourth-century historian Ephorus of Kyme tell of a special connection between Kyme and Phrygia due to the harbor; as a coastal site, Kyme would prove a useful friend to landlocked Phrygia. In fact, tradition continues, the daughter of the Phrygian king Midas—famous for his golden touch—was given in marriage to one Agamemnon of Kyme. Another demonstration of Kyme's seafaring is Cumae, in Italy, said to be a joint colony founded in the later eighth century by people of Kyme and of Chalkis on Euboea.[15] We remember that the poet's father left Kyme, needful of a good life, and traveled over the wide sea in a black ship. Perhaps, in the spirit of an epigram preserved in the pseudo-Herodotean *Life of Homer,* he realized, "My dear limbs yearn not to stay in the sacred streets of Kyme, but rather my great heart urges me to go unto another country."[16]

And what of grievous Askra and its environs? Was there, in fact, an actual village of this name in the late eighth and early seventh centuries BCE? Results of an extended archaeological survey in Boeotia suggest that an affirmative answer is in order.[17] Survey archaeology is directed not toward

14. S. Mitchell, "Archaeology in Asia Minor, 1979–84," 80.

15. F. Jacoby, *Die Fragmente der Griechischen Historiker,* fragment 534 T1.

16. Evelyn-White, *Hesiod,* 469.

17. See John Bintliff, "Reflections on Nine Years with the Bradford-Cambridge Boeotia Project."

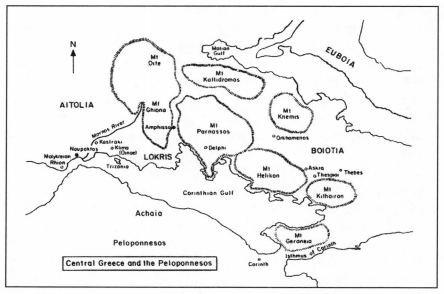

Map of Boeotia showing the region of Askra. (With permission of John M. Fossey)

excavation of a particular site, but rather toward intensive examination of the surface of a region in order to understand the interaction between humans and the environment. In this examination, location of a range of settlements is a prominent feature. Following the description of the site of Askra given by Strabo, who located its ruins "to the right of Helikon" and "forty stades [about 7.5 kilometers] distant from Thespiai," members of the project carried out an organized investigation of the territory (*Geography,* trans. Jones, 1927, 9.2.25). In the course of the study they discovered house walls, remains of a possible circuit wall, and an extraordinarily high density of surface artifacts extending over an area of about sixty acres at the foot of a hill known as Pyrgaki.

Pyrgaki is not an acropolis of the height of those at Athens or Corinth; rather, it is an easy climb of less than fifteen minutes. Still, the view from its summit gives a good panorama of a long valley, oriented east to west, known even today as the Valley of the Muses. Earliest indications of settlement at the site identified as Askra date to the late eleventh or early tenth century. Meagerness of surviving evidence from the tenth through the

The Valley of the Muses from Pyrgaki. (Photograph by Richard R. Johnson and used with his permission)

eighth centuries suggests a small farming village, a status that would ac-cord with the view that neighboring Thespiai was the dominant town in the region. The land is rocky, but small springs are abundant. The region "includes some excellent farming-land and is in particular the prime vine-growing area within the former territory of the polis of Thespiai." Other travelers to the region have sought the rivers, springs, and mountains mentioned in the poems. Hippokrene has been identified with a spring now called Kryopegadi, just below the summit of Mount Zagaras on the north side. It is, according to Paul Wallace, "a delightful place" that coincides nicely with the description of it by Pausanias.[18] The Permessos has been equated with the modern stream Archontitsa and the Olmeios with the stream flowing down from Agios Christos.

18. A. M. Snodgrass, "The Site of Askra," 93; Wallace, "Hesiod and the Valley of the Muses," 8.

Spring in the rocky slopes of "miserable" Askra. (Photograph by Richard R. Johnson and used with his permission)

The heights of Helikon and the Valley of the Muses have had sacral associations from antiquity to the present. Not only remains from antiquity but also a number of Christian chapels indicate the enduring sanctity of the region. In light of the lasting attachment of reverence to particular places in Greek tradition, it is not difficult to imagine an altar of Zeus (*Theogony* 4) becoming a chapel of Agios Elias on the summit of Mount Zagaras above the spring of Hippokrene. In similar fashion, places sacred to the Muses could assume another form of sanctity, just as Athena's Parthenon, for example, came to be the Cathedral of Our Lady of Athens.

Thebes, a Mycenaean center, experienced a continuous existence through the Dark Age to flourish as the leading polis of Boeotia in the classical period. Archaeology demonstrates that Aulis, too, had a Mycenaean physical presence as well as a legendary identification as the point of departure for the Greek fleet setting sail for Troy.[19] In that same capacity, it was the place where King Agesilaus of Sparta offered a sacrifice before launching his own expedition to Asia Minor. The polis of Chalkis gained fame in the later Dark Age as the home of intrepid traders and colonizers expanding horizons beyond their immediate territory of Euboea. Thucydides included Chalkis in his account of early times in the context of interpolis strife: "The nearest approach to a coalition took place in the old war between Chalkis and Eretria; this was a quarrel in which the rest of the Hellenic name did to some extent take sides" (1.15, trans. Crawley). The towns shared the fertile Lelantine Plain but, at some point in the late eighth or early seventh century, went to war in order to gain full control of the land. It was to Chalkis that Hesiod journeyed to participate in games for "warlike Amphidamas," whose sons established the games and set up many prizes (lines 654–55). According to Plutarch, Amphidamas had been killed while distinguishing himself in a sea battle between the two neighboring towns (*Moralia* 153–54). Hesiod is not too modest to announce that he won the prize of a tripod with his song.

The Land and the Sea

People and places form the backdrop to the most important subject of *Works and Days,* which is often described as an ancient *Farmer's Almanac:* more than 50 percent of the poem deals directly with farming and animal husbandry. In the poet's opinion, the best work for mortals is associated with the land. Hesiod's advice begins with general observations: work so that your granary will be filled with sustenance (lines 300–301); order your work according to the seasons (304–5); do not acquire—that is, grab—goods through shameful means (320–27); have reverence for the gods (336–41); and deal with people—even a brother—wisely and with caution (370–72). At line 383, the advice becomes specific: "When the Pleiades, daughters of Atlas, rise, begin to harvest but when they set, start to plant." The working year divides into three broad seasons: fall (383–492), winter (493–563), and spring (564–617). "In the season of exhausting

19. Vasilis Aravantinos, ephor of preclassical and classical antiquities in Boeotia, expressed this opinion in September 2000 when he graciously exhibited recent archaeological work in Thebes. On Aulis, see Simpson, *Mycenaean Greece,* 53, entry B53.

summer . . . one can drink the shining wine while sitting in the shade"
(584, 592–93).

A farmer's year is directed by the pattern of the stars.[20] The appearance and disappearance of the Pleiades define the proper times to prepare the soil and to harvest its fruits. The setting of the Pleiades signals
the time for serious plowing (mid-November). At that time you must
sharpen the iron of your plow, prepare other equipment, and ready your
oxen and helpers for work. Immediately after the Pleiades give the signal, begin to rise early and work, all of you, even in wet weather. After
plowing, plant during the winter season of rain. During the cold months
of winter, by contrast, take good care of your beasts, for the wind goes
through the hide of an ox and a goat, and it drives an old man to running (515–19). Keep indoors, paying attention to your home, but if you
must go out-of-doors, remember your cape, shoes, and felt hat. When
Arcturus begins to rise (566–67), it is time to prune your vines (late February). With the return of the Pleiades after they have spent forty days
"hiding" (May), you should undertake your harvest. Then, winnow Dem-
eter's yield when Orion appears (June) and store it carefully (597–601).
Fallow plowing in the summer is beneficial. Cut your grapes when Orion
and Sirius are in the middle of the sky (September); after showing the
grapes to the sun for ten days and nights, cover them for five more days,
then press out the juice (609–14).

Quite specific instruction follows in the remainder of the poem's calendar of days (695–826): when and whom to marry, relationships with other
people, and regard for the blessed immortals, concluding (from line 765)
with a list of activities appropriate and inappropriate to certain days. Both
the eleventh and twelfth days of the month, for instance, are excellent for
shearing sheep and gathering the fruits of the earth that gladden the heart.
But the twelfth is far better than the eleventh since on that day the spider
spins its web in the full light of day and the ant gathers its heap. Some
days are better in the morning, others in the afternoon; certain days are
good for boys but bad for girls.

The calendar accords well with the agricultural year of classical Greece

---

20. West includes information in his commentary to the text (*Hesiod*, esp. 252–56) and
in "Excursus II, Time-Reckoning" (376–81).

and with modern Greek agriculture.[21] Certainly, there have been innovations in crops and technology since the seventh century BCE: cotton and tobacco have been introduced, horses have replaced oxen as draft animals, and irrigation plays a far more important role in use of the land today. However, in Boeotia grains, grapes, and olives continue to be major crops. Beehives dot the slopes, and sheep, goats, mules, and dogs are as familiar now as they were in Hesiod's Askra. Even those who believe that Hesiod is a construct of oral poetry realize the correspondence of the information in the poem with actual farming in preclassical Greece.[22] Study of the environment over time demonstrates the essential continuity of landform, climate, and water supply.[23] Because the environment is the major factor in ways that the land can be effectively used, continuity of land use is to be expected. Thus, the activities and calendar described in *Works and Days* are well suited to the environment and weather patterns of mainland Greece, more particularly to central Greece where Askra is located.

The farmer as portrayed by Hesiod does far more than raise crops and tend herds: he cares for his animals, gelding boars and bulls on the eighth of the month and mules on the twelfth (790–91); he constructs and maintains his equipment (420–36) and buildings on his land—the sixth day of the month is suitable for putting an enclosure around a sheep pen (787); he fashions shoes, capes, and hats (540–46); and his wife weaves cloth at her loom—the twelfth day of the month is best for setting up a loom (779). Even the account of the respite that summer offers evokes the life of a farmer: when the artichoke flowers and the cricket sings is the time for

21. Robin Osborne, *Classical Landscape with Figures: The Ancient Greek City and Its Countryside*, 13–14; Peter Walcot, *Greek Peasants, Ancient and Modern*, esp. chap. 2, "Labour and Agriculture" (25–44).

22. Lamberton concludes that "we have good reason to believe that Hesiod's calendar corresponds to the realities of farming in pre-classical Greece" (*Hesiod*, 129).

23. "The Mediterranean climate, though apparently remarkably stable over the past four thousand years, is never totally static. . . . [Yet] the evidence seems to indicate that we can postulate with fair confidence the essential continuity of conditions like soil, climate, and water supply that are the basic determinants in agricultural regions" (William A. Mc-Donald and George R. Rapp Jr., *The Minnesota Messenia Expedition: Reconstructing a Bronze Age Regional Environment,* 251). Although this conclusion derives from extensive survey in the southwestern Peloponnese, it is applicable to most of southern and central mainland Greece.

sitting in the shade drinking shining wine, without forgetting, of course, to make four libations and enjoy a curd cake along with some meat (582–96).[24]

Intertwined with the practical instruction on farming is the poet's counsel on attitude and behavior. Full barns are necessary, he enjoins, if you enjoy wasting time listening to the quarrels at the meeting place (29–31), and you will not fill your barn by avoiding labor (411–12). But take care: a full barn may lure a designing woman (373–74). The poet leaves no doubt that work on the land is backbreaking, but it is the best way to gain a livelihood. In the golden age, mortals lived peacefully tending their fields; they were rich in flocks and dear to the immortal gods (118–20), but that age is long gone.

Hesiod also knows that men take to the sea and even offers instructions about the proper times to sail and the cargo to carry. These instructions begin at line 618, on the chance that "desire for rough seafaring seizes you." The poet describes the two seasons when seafaring is possible: the fifty days following the summer solstice and in spring when leaves at the very top of the fig tree are as large as a crow's footprint. One should never venture out to sea when the Pleiades are hiding themselves. At that time, tend to your ship and its equipment. When you do fill your ship with cargo, remember that the greater cargo brings the greater profits. Yet, the advice continues, do not trust all your livelihood to a hollow ship, but leave the larger part onshore, gambling on the smaller portion. "You will escape grief only with great difficulty" (684).

Agriculture has been the main occupation and source of livelihood in Greece from the Neolithic age well into the twentieth century. And when Greek culture flourishes, seafaring is a strong ingredient. Consequently, we must admit that a general recital of the need to work hard to control the difficult terrain of most of Greece along with advice to take to the sea do not locate Hesiod's advice in a particular time frame. Even with that warning, it is instructive to remember that the eighth century witnessed a marked increase in seafaring after a long inability or reluctance to take to

---

24. In his doctoral dissertation, "Dancing Zeus: Leisure and Society in Archaic and Classical Greece," Zinon Papakonstantinou describes the image as a "bucolic scene of solitary drinking" that contrasts markedly with the aristocratic economy of leisure of the Homeric society (46).

Poseidon's realm, and with that development agricultural life underwent significant changes that had major repercussions in all levels of society. More-over, as we will see, other clues in the poems significantly narrow the temporal horizon.

Other Problems

Other stresses than the constant, backbreaking need to work the poor soil exist in Hesiod's Askra. Not everyone is content to work: some seize their wealth or steal it by the cleverness of their tongues (321–22), an action as wicked as wronging a guest or suppliant, bedding a brother's wife, offending fatherless children, or abusing an elderly father (327–32). Even Perses has seized what was not rightfully his. The brothers divided the family land upon the death of their father, but Perses seized the greater portion or perhaps many other things such as tools and furniture[25] by fueling (with gifts) the pride of the gift-devouring lords, who delight in judging according to this sort of "right. Fools that they are!" (37–41). It is best to have a single son in a household (376), for then the land will not be divided. If there are two brothers, they must deal with one another. So, Hesiod advises, "when you deal with your brother, be pleasant, but get a witness" (371). Even then it may result that your brother is no longer your friend as he was in the old days (184).

Personality clashes arise in many families for scores of reasons, but a single widespread condition created an atmosphere of tension throughout much of Greece in the eighth century. Population was increasing considerably, and, as numbers of inhabitants rose, available land became inadequate. As farming or herding or both constituted the economic base of livelihood, competition for land—even marginal land—gained intensity. Two alternatives existed for farmers and their communities: to encroach upon the land of neighbors (seizing it, Hesiod would say) or to look farther afield for less densely populated areas. Early Greek history attests both courses: the struggle over land of neighboring communities and the outpouring to establish homes away from Greece that begins about 750 and continues for two centuries, resulting in a band of Greek communities around much of the coast of the Mediterranean and Black Seas.

25. On the interpretation of the meaning of the Greek, see the discussion in Peter Green, "Works and Days 1–285: Hesiod's Invisible Audience," 27–28.

Although he has painful words about the difficulties of farming and the disasters involved in dividing estates, his chosen course is to try to wrest a livelihood from his portion of the family land. Yet he knows of transplanting firsthand: his father, unable to escape from poverty by continuing to farm a plot in Kyme, took to the sea perhaps originally to trade but eventually to settle into the burg he calls Askra.

Another contributor to the land shortage and the tension it produced was concentration of holdings in the hands of the few more privileged members of communities. Differentiation in status is evident even in earlier Dark Age communities where, as at Nichoria in the southern Peloponnese and at Lefkandi on Euboea, one larger dwelling set amid other smaller houses contained greater quantities of goods that were also of higher quality.[26] By the eighth century, however, several families had been successful in garnering wealth, expressed primarily in more extensive estates but also through profits obtained by trade.

David Tandy argues convincingly, in *Warriors into Traders,* that a population increase of approximately threefold led to a radical transformation of economic institutions in the eighth century: "[T]he redistributive and reciprocal system in which all people were assured of livelihoods (graded by people's position in society) was replaced by a system in which markets were important to survival, perhaps even crucial."[27] It was the existing elite who could take advantage of new opportunities, for they would have a surplus to exchange for other goods, often luxury goods in the first phases of reviving trade. Through their activity, the participants gained wealth, and, what is just as important, that wealth was unobligated by constraints of the rules of the existing redistributive economy of their communities. According to the earlier nature of trade, mutual obligations governed exchange between a center marked by the chief's presence and the households of the periphery. The consequences of the change altered the rules of the game, as unobligated wealth led to the emergence of private property, debt, an ability to transfer land, and conflict over land use. The cumulative result was felt throughout the social, political, and economic systems.

---

26. See Thomas and Conant, *From Citadel to City-State.*
27. Tandy, *Warriors into Traders,* 2, 85, 136.

This same century saw the gradual enlargement of communal bound-aries, as settlements that were once separate drew—or were drawn—together for economic, social, political, and military purposes. In defining communal territory, boundary formation "is likely to have encouraged a gradual strengthening of individual property rights."[28] Those already priv-ileged in their landholdings were in a position to benefit by the formaliza-tion of property rights. Their incipient political status is also likely to have increased. Evidence from Corinth and Athens particularly indicates the emergence of formal offices and collegial boards for direction of commu-nal activities in the early archaic period. In Corinth, traditional kingship ended around 750, when management of community affairs passed into the hands of a clan known as the Bacchiadae. A single official chosen from this clan held office for one year, while a council of all Bacchiad heads of family deliberated the full range of matters associated with the collective well-being. In Athens, according to Aristotle's *Constitution of the Athenians,* the rule of one was put in commission of three individual offices, and some decades later (around 650) a body of six law setters (*thesmothetai*) was added to the official positions of the polis. In sum, land brought position as well as wealth: Greece at the start of the seventh century was an aristoc-racy of those privileged by wealth and status.

What is the societal order in Hesiod's poems? *Basileis* is the title ac-corded the heads of these fortunate families, and Hesiod knows the ways of these "lords" well: "O Basileis," he cautions. "Do you yourselves ponder / this kind of Dike! And being present among mankind / the immortals observe those who with crooked judgments / oppress others fearing the wrath of the gods not one whit" (248–51). "Be on your guard, lords, ren-der straight judgments, / you gift devourers, turn away completely from crooked judgments" (263–64). Apart from his words of complaint to the lords and to Perses, Hesiod has no solution to the perceived injustice. He hopes that Zeus will intervene (273).

We must acknowledge that the situation in Askra may have been unusual. Yet other evidence from the seventh century suggests that concentration of

28. C. H. Lyttkens, "The Origins of the Polis: An Economic Perspective on Institutional Change in Ancient Greece, 1000–600 B.C.," 12. On consolidation, see Walter Donlan, "The Pre-state Community in Greece" and "The Relations of Power in the Pre-state and Early State Politics."

wealth and power in the hands of few had become the rule in many communities and was now a growing dilemma throughout much of the Greek
world. One of the first uses of alphabetic literacy in service of the communal well-being was codification of law, which was well under way by the
mid-seventh century. The content of those early codes defines the rules of
conduct and the means for deciding cases where those rules have been
broken. One of the most prominent areas of concern is ownership and
disposition of property. In a society primarily dependent upon produce
from the land, this prominence in the early codes is to be expected.[29]
Although disputes arose between individuals, solutions involved the entire community and were carried out in public.

Perhaps the best-known example is the dispute pictured on the shield
that Hephaistos designs for Achilles in the *Iliad:*

> The people were gathered in the meeting place. For a quarrel
> had erupted, and two men were quarreling over the blood price
> for a slain man. One promised publicly to pay the full amount
> but the other refused to accept anything.
> Both then put it to an arbitrator to make a decision;
> and people were applauding both sides, helping both men.
> But the heralds restrained the people, while the elders
> Remained seated on their polished stones in the sacred circle.
>
> (18.497–504)

Less detailed but strikingly similar is Hesiod's advice that it is unwise to
hang about listening to the disputes in the agora; one who does not have
sufficient grain stored at home has no time for disputes and matters of the
agora (29–30). Besides, this Strife is heavy to bear βαρύς, by contrast with
her sister—the other Strife—who is far better πολλόν ἀμείνω for mankind. "Heavy" Strife gave birth to Toil, Forgetfulness, Famine, tearful Sorrows,
Fights, Battles, Murders, Manslaughters, Quarrels, Lying Words, Disputes,

---

29. Primacy in codification seems to belong to Crete. "It looks as if every Cretan city
had got some sort of civil code published before the end of the sixth century at latest; and
since the earliest parts of the Dreros code . . . look to be of the seventh, probably the larger
cities like Gortyn or Knossos published them equally early, though their earliest surviving
inscribed blocks belong to the sixth century" (Jeffery, *Archaic Greece,* 188–89). On areas of
concern, see Michael Gagarin, *Early Greek Law,* 63, 139.

Lawlessness, Ruin, and Oath ὅρκος "who brings the most harm to earth-bound men when anyone of them willingly swears a false oath" (*Theogony* 226–32).

As we have seen, Hesiod understands the harm firsthand; if the evidence of *Works and Days* is to be trusted, one of those quarrelsome disputes involved Hesiod and Perses. "In the past," Hesiod says, "we divided our family lot, but in your grasping way you took more, / feeding the pride of the lords, / gift devourers that they are, who enjoy making decisions according to this kind of justice. / Fools they are, who do not know how much better is half than the whole / and how much good there is in mallow and asphodel" (37–41). "Now," he pleads, "let us decide our quarrel by ourselves / according to straight justice, the best kind of judgments that come from Zeus" (35–36).

Fact or Fiction?

A substantial picture of an individual and his world emerges from the poems. Even so, Richmond Lattimore's caveat is worth remembering: although "the proem to the *Theogony* . . . makes it clear that Hesiod wrote this poem also . . . deliberate forgery is, of course, possible. It always is." Even the accord between the two prefaces may be irrelevant to a search for the poet if, as some have suggested, they are later additions to the poems. Robert Lamberton suspects that their transmission along with the rest of the poems "is a function of *the idea* of Hesiod that was current at the time when we can first credibly maintain that written copies proliferated—the Hellenistic period." He finds further proof of the actual singer of the prefaces in line 35: "But what is all of this about oak and stone to me?" Here, Lamberton argues, "Hesiod explodes his own myth, throws down the shepherd's mask, and exposes that persona for what it is—a charming poetic convention of an old-fashioned sort, a fairy tale. . . . What does this sort of discourse have to do with me—oaks and rocks? What need do I have to adopt an old-fashioned style?"[30] In other words, such a view would continue the tradition of anonymous singers from the late Dark Age through the classical period and into the Hellenistic age.

30. Lattimore, trans., *Hesiod*, 4; Lamberton, *Hesiod*, 47–48, 63.

Much of the doubt over the identification of Hesiod as a person rather than a persona assumed by a series of anonymous bards stems from questions associated with the Homeric epics. An enduring aspect of the "Homeric question" concerns authorship: was there, in fact, a Homer, or is this simply a title assumed by all those who continued the oral tradition of the tale of Troy? J. A. K. Thomson announces plainly, "That Homer is no more than a type, the representative of all minstrels who preserved the poetry passing under his name, must, I think, be accepted by any one who gives the most obvious interpretation to certain things which we know to be true of the ancient Greek epos."[31]

Joined to the issue of the historicity of Homer is the question of the epics associated with that name. In 1795, Friedrich A. Wolf asked in *Prolegomena to Homer* whether writing was known at the time the *Iliad* was composed. Concluding that it was not, he demonstrated that the epics were the products of oral tradition. Moreover, their sheer bulk would have made it impossible for anyone to recite them in their entirely. Thus, Wolf decided, only small independent poems existed until they were gathered together into the unified epics that we now have. That occasion occurred, according to Wolf, in the sixth century when the Athenian tyrant Peisistratos appointed a commission for this compilation in connection with the rhapsodic contests in the Panathenaic festival. Fueled by these intertwined views, the conclusion gathered supporters well into the twentieth century. Moreover, it led to doubts about other bards, especially those whose verse had strong characteristics of the oral tradition. Writing just fourteen years ago, Lamberton asserted that "Hesiod . . . is even more susceptible than Homer to reclassification as collective expression rather than original talent."[32]

An understanding of the oral tradition puts the issue of creative genius in clearer focus. It is true that the durability of oral tradition necessitates multiple singers performing traditional tales over long periods of time. In seeking the possibility of an Ur-*Argonautica,* for example, I have posited a span stretching over eight hundred years. Most of those singers are anonymous in oral traditions generally, not simply in the case of Greek traditions. "The products of an oral culture serve communal interests: they remember

---

31. Thomson, *Studies in the Odyssey,* 189.
32. Lamberton, *Hesiod,* 22.

information essential to and imbedded in the workings of the community for they are conditioned by interests of the community of which they are members." Even so, the process allows—more likely requires—especially creative singers, and, in fact, oral poetry grants great potential freedom to singers: though owing form and substance to earlier songs, each performance of a song depends upon the skills of its singer. As evidence from modern oral cultures shows, certain individuals with natural abilities for song become, through training, specialists in the memory of their culture's tradition. The studies of Milman Parry and Albert B. Lord in Yugoslavian oral tradition discovered Avdo Medjedovíc who, like Homer, "sang traditional songs . . . of extraordinary quality."[33]

The power of the epic narrative of the "Homeric" poems is beyond question, and a uniquely gifted singer is often seen as the source of that power. We may name that singer "Homer," as the ancient Greeks did, or we may (perversely?) assign another name to the bard responsible for "codifying" the strands of a long tradition centering on the Trojan War. During the past half century, use of the name Homer has recovered acceptability.

The case for Hesiod differs somewhat. Though the form of *Works and Days* and *Theogony* is akin to Homeric epic hexameter, and, in fact, their dialect is the Ionian epic *koine,* also akin to Homeric, Hesiod may be at the beginning of a new convention rather than near the end of a long-standing tradition. Near Eastern roots of several elements of Hesiod's poems are clear—the Myth of the Ages in *Works and Days* and the Succession Myth in *Theogony* are particularly notable. A strong case can be made for an eighth-century date of borrowing, a period when contacts between the Greek world and the Near East were quickening after a long period of little interaction.[34] Hesiod is the earliest of three names associated with Greek gnomic poetry, the other two being Phocylides and Theognis, both dated to the mid-sixth century or rather later. A memory tradition dating back to the early seventh century remembers the first Greek poet, namely, Hesiod, associated by name with gnomic verse. It is significant that Hesiod's father is reported to have come to the mainland from Kyme in Asia Minor

---

33. Vansina, "Oral Tradition as Process," 108; Lord, "Characteristics of Orality," 62. See also M. Parry, A. B. Lord, and D. E. Bynum, *Serbo Croatian Heroic Songs.*

34. Peter Walcot, *Hesiod and the Near East,* 118–23.

where contact with non-Greek Anatolian peoples was well under way in the ninth century.

That he was remembered by means of written word rather than solely by oral tradition may strengthen such a view. Literacy returned to Greece in the eighth century, in the form of alphabetic writing; currently, the earliest surviving inscriptions date to around 770 BCE. A case has been made that the Homeric poems were among the first long works preserved in written form.[35] Unfortunately, Hesiod's position in the newly literate culture of Greece is uncertain. He describes himself as a simple shepherd who was inspired by the Muses—in other words, a bard who composed within the techniques of oral poetry. And, as we have seen, *Theogony* and *Works and Days* are formulaic hexameter verses.

If we place him in the period around 700, when alphabetic writing was spreading in the Greek world, Hesiod may also have written his verses, although he does not mention writing. David Tandy believes that *Works and Days* was "written down from the start." The outspoken criticism of the "lords" of Askra, Tandy argues, necessitates freedom from the patronage of those lords, inasmuch as the epic poems clearly reveal the patronage role of the *aristoi* in performance of song. "Effective criticism must avoid the big man and be good. Only writing meets both demands, for oral poetry is at its best only when in the presence of immediate reward. Written poetry may be good without this consideration."[36]

This position does not erase the oral elements of the poems. Martin West's position is sensible: "[I]t is a natural supposition that much of the material embodied in the *Works and Days* had been used by Hesiod in oral recitations. . . . It is not to be supposed that having written a poem down Hesiod ceased to recite it, or that he abstained from reciting it in the middle of writing it down."[37]

---

35. On the early inscriptions, see M. R. Popham, L. H. Sackett, and P. G. Themelis, eds., *Lefkandi I: The Iron Age,* 89; on the date of written Homeric poems, see H. T. Wade-Gery, *The Poet of the Iliad,* and, more recently, Barry Powell, *Homer and the Origin of the Greek Alphabet.*

36. Tandy, *Warriors into Traders,* 200. See also "An Antiaristocratic Tradition?" (194–201). "The critical portions of *Works and Days* . . . I have to conclude must have been composed and distributed in writing, for I cannot convince myself of any other explanation" (214 n. 108).

37. West, *Hesiod,* 59. Sinclair assumes Hesiod's literacy: "The author did not use verse because he was writing poetry, but because verse was the only known medium. He did not

How knowledge of the alphabet reached Askra is not known. I wonder, however, whether one piece of autobiographical information may not offer a clue. The father of Hesiod and Perses was born in Kyme in Asia Minor, a settlement that was well known for its early seafaring. Dios—if this is his name—left Kyme, needful as he was of a good life, and sought that good life from the sea. To explain the situation in which Greeks gained knowledge of the Semitic alphabet, many suggest that contact between traders is the most likely scenario. Kevin Robb has re-created such a meeting when "some clever Greek . . . was listening to a friendly Phoenician recite the Semitic abecedarium. . . . Much patience was required on the part of the instructing Phoenician, as no doubt again and again the Greek and his instructor went over the signs in order, first pronouncing the sounds they suggested to the Semitic ear and then finding the closest approximation for the Greek ear."[38] Dios may have been one of the clever Greeks, even though an argument for Hesiod's literacy does not depend on this possibility.

Thus, rather than projecting the poet several hundreds of years later in time to the Hellenistic age, we might be wise to remember the view of the classical Greeks. Herodotus's mention of Hesiod states that Homer and Hesiod lived no more than four hundred years before his own time, which was the mid-fifth century. Although he offers no date, he describes the temple of Zeus at Nemea as the place where the poet Hesiod is said to have been killed, obviously well before his own time (3.96.1). Construction of temples began in the eighth century, and although the temple of Zeus at Nemea dates to the sixth century, remains of an earlier *heroön* have been discovered there.

So let us keep the places and name of the *prooemia,* at least for the present, while investigating the value of additional "biographical" details in the body of *Works and Days.* Does the picture agree with the Greek view that a man named Hesiod, living sometime earlier than Herodotus, created these two poems? To respond to this question requires critical consideration of several lines of reasoning that seem to yield a negative answer.

---

use hexameters because he was writing epic, but because it was the only metre he knew. . . . The author began to write a series of admonitions, and such was his enthusiasm for his subject that he almost succeeded in writing a fine poem" (*Hesiod,* xi).

38. Robb, *Literacy and Paideia in Ancient Greece,* 272–73.

One position dismisses the actuality of the advice presented in *Works and Days*. It is an "account of the world that plays at belonging to a dusty little Boeotian town some 2500 years ago." The advice is generic, capturing much of the spirit of any agricultural community. On the other hand, Stephanie A. Nelson believes that the impression that the poet is following the farmer's year is illusory; in fact, she finds that much of the chronology of the annual round of work is inexplicable. What is more, "there is nothing in Hesiod's advice that anyone from such a background would not already have known." Not a farmer's manual, rather the poem "is teaching us what the cycle of the year, with its balance of summer and winter, of good and evil, of profit and risk, of anxiety and relaxation, implies about the will of Zeus."

Such a conclusion may weaken one of the supports for Hesiod's historicity, but it need not do so. In fact, Nelson concludes that the poet is "who he says he is": "the simplest explanation for Hesiod's deep and all-pervasive concern with farming is that he was, in fact, a farmer."[39] To be sure, he is concerned with the will of Zeus; he uses his world and experience in it to press that concern. In addition to the larger subject of the farming work that Zeus admires, Hesiod's world constantly insinuates itself into the verses. We learn that it was shared with spiders, ants, worms, snails, cranes, hawks, nightingales, swallows, crows, and bees and that four-footed members included oxen, mules, sheep, horses, goats, dogs, and boars.

In response to the assertion that Hesiod's poems are little more than proverbial wisdom, it is necessary to note that the earliest Greek poetry is generally fond of proverbial wisdom, even when attribution to known poets is secure. "The fruit of youth is a moment" (Mimnermos); "One of the finest things the man from Chios said: The generations of men are like the generations of leaves" (Semonides); "No man ever proves himself a good man in war unless he can endure to face the blood and the slaughter" (Theognis); "For Gyges gold I do not care, I do not envy him or dare high *tyrannis,* far from my eyes are things like this" (Archilochus); "Fate brings humanity her good; she brings him her evil; and what the gods give

---

39. Lamberton, *Hesiod,* 101. In his study *Greek Peasants,* Walcot defines Hesiod as "a classic example of the peasant" (15) and his world as representative of agricultural villages generally, in both the nature of work and values. Nelson, *God and the Land: The Metaphysics of Farming in Hesiod and Vergil,* 50, 57, 31–32, 39.

us for gifts no man can refuse" (Solon). In this light, "What is this talk of oak and stone to me?" may be better understood by the usual interpretation offered by Hugh G. Evelyn-White in his note to the line in the Loeb edition: "A proverbial saying meaning, 'why enlarge on irrelevant topics?'"[40] Or put another way, the relevant topic is the Muses and Zeus, *not* the human taught to sing by the daughters of mighty Zeus.

Moreover, the context of the poem's advice enfolded into reflections on farming points to conditions in Greece during what has been called the "age of revolution," that is, the century between 750 and 650 BCE. As noted previously, agriculture has been the foundation of Greek economy from the time of the first settled villages around 7000 BCE into the twentieth century.[41] However, a profound change was occurring at the time when linguistic evidence dates the composition of Hesiod's poems. Whereas basic subsistence farming had been nearly the total mainstay of life during the four hundred years of the Dark Age, diversification grew stronger and more varied during the eighth century as conditions in the Aegean region became more stable. Some find evidence for improvement in climatic conditions, whereas others believe that new tools, particularly the iron plowshare, increased agricultural productivity, which, in turn, led to a rapid growth in population.[42] As numbers of inhabitants rose, many areas of Greece experienced a shortage of land, so competition for land—even marginal land—gained intensity. The two alternatives were to acquire land adjacent to one's community or to relocate to regions were land suitable for agriculture was available. The Spartans managed to seize all of neighboring Messenia in their efforts to alleviate land shortage, whereas many communities traveled across the sea to found a new community (a home away, or *apoikia*) where life would be more secure than it had been in

40. Evelyn-White, *Hesiod,* 81 n. 1.

41. Even in the increasingly urban culture of the twentieth century, 43 percent of the Greek labor force was still employed in agricultural activities in 1970. "Greece remains still a nation of villages" (Walcot, *Greek Peasants,* 25).

42. Thomas and Conant, *From Citadel to City-State,* 37. On climate, see Jan Bouzek, *Greece, Anatolia, and Europe: Cultural Interrelations during the Early Iron Age,* 20–21. The pattern Bouzek sketches finds recovery from severe drought around 1000, followed by a cycle of poor crops lasting into the ninth century when signs of recovery are evident. A new period of drought in the second half of the eighth century was a factor in the widespread colonization beginning at that time.

Greece. Hesiod does not reflect on the possibility of joining a group to found an *apoikia,* but he does recall his father's resettlement from Kyme to Askra. And he has experienced the result of one of the struggles between two communities on the island of Euboea. His one distant adventure was to travel to Chalkis on the island of Euboea to participate in funeral games for its *basileus* Amphidamas who was killed in a long war with the neighboring community of Eretria over ownership of the fertile plain that lay between them. It was here that he won the tripod for his song that some suggest was *Theogony* (*Works and Days,* 651–58).

Another contributor to the land shortage and the tension it produced was concentration of holdings in the hands of the few more privileged members of communities. As mentioned above, differentiation in status is evident even in the early Dark Age communities. By the eighth century, evidence—particularly that from burials—indicates an increase in the number of individuals and families who had been successful in garnering wealth.[43] Much of that wealth came from the produce of their estates, but this foundation provided the means to engage in the newly burgeoning trade, a subject that raises another objection to the historical value of the poem.

But what, some have asked, would anyone from landlocked Askra have to do with the sea? "Seafaring is an afterthought, and attempts to establish that a farmer from a dusty corner of Boeotia, hours from salt water, would in fact go off on commercial sailing ventures after the grain harvest are utterly unconvincing."[44]

An answer to that question requires consideration of the developments affecting the larger Greek world at the end of the eighth century and the start of the seventh, the "Age of Revolution."[45] The view that communities in mainland Greece were virtually isolated from the larger Aegean and Mediterranean spheres throughout most of the Dark Age is no longer accurate. During the earlier part of that period, inhabitants of the mainland traveled eastward to the coast of Asia Minor and into the waters of the

43. See Morris, *Archaeology and Cultural History,* esp. chap. 6. "As members of the ninth-century elite asserted the prominence of their dead more aggressively, so too they defined membership of their group more rigorously" (253).

44. Lamberton, *Hesiod,* 131.

45. Chester Starr deserves credit for the term and its dating to roughly 750–650 or, "to hazard greater precision, principally in the brief decades from 720–680" (*The Origins of Greek Civilization: 1100–750 B.C.,* 381).

eastern Mediterranean, particularly to Cyprus. By the ninth century, contact between Greece and the Near East was resumed.

Adventurers from Euboea were among the earliest travelers to Cyprus and the Levant. Their activity is well represented by exports found on Cyprus and Al Mina in Syria. In fact, some are persuaded that Euboeans may have been the original settlers of Al Mina, which was to become one of the leading trading centers of the Levant.[46] The new skill of alphabetic writing adapted from a Phoenician alphabet is also associated with Euboea. Euboean travelers sailed northward as well to establish trade in the northern Aegean in the ninth century, and in the following century their presence was established in Italy, first on the offshore island of Ischia where Pithecoussai was founded as early as 770 and later (around 725) at Cumae on the west coast of the Italian peninsula. Euboean presence on Sicily was also established in the last third of the eighth century at Naxos, Leontini, Katane, and Zancle, which had the reputation of beginning as a pirates' nest.[47] Across the strait on the toe of Italy, they planted Rhegion. All of these five settlements date from between roughly 734 and 720. It is with good reason that Euboea is described as "famed for its ships" in the Homeric "Hymn to Apollo" and that names of people in the family of the Euboean hero Palamedes are associated with the sea: a brother is "Tiller" (Oiax); his father, "Shipman" (Nauplios); grandfather, "Famed-for-ships" (Klutoneos); and great-grandfather, "Ship-launcher" (Naubolos).[48]

The precociousness of the Euboeans infected others. In fact, from 750

46. R. A. Kearsley argues that "the very first settlers at Al Mina, around the mid-8th century, were a group of Greek mercenaries" ("Greeks Overseas in the 8th Century B.C.," 119). Considerable debate exists about the primacy of the Euboeans in early trade and colonization. For a challenge to the case for Euboean entrepreneurship, see John K. Papadopoulos, "Phantom Euboeans." The title of the article may be unfortunate: though Euboean activity may be overstated by some, it cannot be dismissed as a "phantom."

47. A ninth-century trading station has been detected at Sindos in the northern Aegean ("Secrets of Sindos," by Michalis A. Tiverios, in excerpts and summaries of translations of articles on archaeological topics in daily Greek newspapers, in Carol Zerner of the American School of Classical Studies for the electronic list Aegeanet, week of September 26–October 2, 1995). The piratical reputation is given in Jeffery, Archaic Greece, 55. Tandy provides a succinct account of Euboean activity in chap. 3, "Early Movements of Goods and of Greeks," of Warriors into Traders (59–78).

48. Apollonius of Rhodes, Argonautica 1.134–38. The translations are those of Carol Dougherty, in The Raft of Odysseus (149), who also presents a catalog of Phaeacian names that are similarly linked to the sea and ships (114).

to 550 an outpouring brought Greeks to new homes extending from the eastern coast of modern Spain to the eastern edge of the Black Sea and, in the southern Mediterranean, the Cyrenaica, west of Egypt. Impetus for the difficult resettlement in communities modeled on those they had left was twofold: acquisition of additional land to support basic subsistence, and access to necessities, especially metals, that Greece could not provide. Trade went hand in hand with settlement. The settlement at Pithecoussai, for example, gave access to the iron resources and products of Etruria.

Archaeological evidence demonstrates that vessels capable of transporting people and goods were available in the eighth century. Of the forty-four representations of ships from the geometric age—from around 900 to 700—forty-three date to about 760 to 710. A deck became common in the eighth century, a significant development in allowing for a second level of rowers, enabling greater speed and providing greater rigidity to the hull. Also during the eighth century, a mortise-and-tenon system for joining the planks replaced the technique of sewing the planks together with cords. The newer technique is far more durable over time or in storm conditions. Ships ranged in size between those that were powered by twenty or fewer rowers to the fifty-oared penteconter. Deck area has been calculated at about 22.5 to 27 square meters for the smaller ships and 60 to 72 square meters for the larger; estimates of hold capacity range from 25 meters cubed to 66 meters cubed. Translated into quantity of cargo that could be carried, these capacities allow 19 tons of grain, or 375 amphoras for the smaller vessels, and 50 tons or 1,000 amphoras for the larger.[49]

Although actual shipwrecks provide testimony of the nature of shipbuilding, much of our evidence comes from vase paintings, which offer another sort of information about the role of ships in eighth-century Greece. After a long absence of objects and people from the repertoire of Greek painters, certain figures begin to return in the later Dark Age. The ship was one of the first images painted on the pottery. "On Geometric

49. On the forty-four representations, see J. S. Morrison and R. T. Williams, *Greek Oared Ships, 900–322 BC*. On the deck, see Wedde, *Ship Imagery*; dating of the evidence "suggests that the double-leveled ship is a Greek invention" (169). On other innovations, see Morrison and Williams, *Greek Oared Ships*, 50; and Dougherty, *The Raft of Odysseus*, 27–29. On the ships' capacity, see Lionel Scott, "Were There Polis Navies in Archaic Greece?" 112–13.

vases, which were decorated with shapes, concentric circles or semicircles, the vase-painter ventured to immortalize only two subjects—the ship and the horse." Ships were also hammered on metal fibulae or modeled; iron spit stands found in a tomb at Argos dating to the eighth century have the form of a long ship.[50] This strong presence of ship motifs surely mirrors the importance of seafaring in the lives of those who produced the objects as well as those who used them.

Skilled not only in the technical craft of ship construction, Greeks of the late Dark Age knew the arts of navigation. The fourth-century accounts of wind observations by Aristotle and Theophrastos—*Meteorologica* and *De Ventris,* respectively—correspond with evidence from the late eighth century. Based on the fourth-century accounts, a calendar[51] assigns the rising of Orion to late June or early July, with Orion's setting in mid- to late November; the winter solstice is dated to December 24 and the summer to June 26; the spring equinox occurs on March 23 and that of autumn on September 26. A conspectus of Hesiod's calendar developed by M. L. West, although less specific in dating, accords well: it fixes Orion's rising in June with the setting in November; the winter solstice occurs in December and the summer in June.[52]

These dates are important in determining suitable times for sailing, which, in Hesiod's instructions, are July and August (663–64) and, slightly less favorable, in April (678–79). From spring into autumn, the manageable westerly winds prevail. "At that time," Hesiod reports, "the winds are steady and the sea is without hostile intent" (670).

William Murray has shown the striking agreement between conditions of the fourth century and the present day, suggesting, consequently, that "modern wind data can be helpful in examining certain aspects of ancient maritime cultures."[53] Since the fourth-century conditions also show strong agreement with conditions of the eighth century, modern data may also be helpful in testing seafaring in the late Dark Age and early archaic period,

50. Else Spathari, *Sailing through Time: The Ship in Greek Art,* 65, 68, 70.

51. Calculated by A. Rehm, "Griechische Kalender. III," and followed by William Murray, "Ancient Sailing Winds in the Eastern Mediterranean: The Case for Cyprus" and "Do Modern Winds Equal Ancient Winds?"

52. West, *Hesiod,* 349–50, 376–81.

53. Murray, "Ancient Sailing Winds," 43.

thereby adding another piece of evidence to a determination of the historicity of Hesiod and his world.

Cynthia Carter and Robert Carter have experienced the waters surrounding Greece for several decades on their sailing vessels of some thirteen meters, approximately the length of Greek ships in the late eighth and seventh centuries. To be sure, the Carters had a motor to aid them when sailing was impossible, but they relied on their "wings," or sails, as the main means of movement. They also learned to appreciate the winds and their seasons. In crossing the Adriatic, they discovered that the wisest course lay between the small island of Othonoi—west of Corfu—and the instep of Italy. Establishment of ports and colonies on Corfu and the instep of Italy tells us that the ancient Greeks were also aware of this path across the Adriatic. With these similarities of winds, ships, and ports, it may not be far-fetched to project experiences of the present back into antiquity. One of the Carters' eastbound crossings took place in mid-August—good westerly conditions. Their point of departure was the harbor of Otranto, just northward around the heel of Italy.

> August 12 we lay in harbor while the wind blew and spray leaped 6 feet above the 20 foot seawall, but on the 13th we reefed down, brought up our anchors, and at 1015 cleared the breakwaters and laid a course for Othonoi. In the early afternoon the coast of Italy faded just as Othonoi appeared ahead, and at 1630 we swept around its SW point in impressive gusts, the air sweet with the scent of herbs, to set two anchors off the beach. While buffeted by gusty wind we feel calm and snug behind the island. 47 miles of fast sailing. . . . On August 14th we had a gentle sail with NW air to Corfu.[54]

Sturdier, faster ships and knowledge of winds and safest courses, reasons to venture beyond the waters of the Aegean, combine to support the evidence of archaeology that travel by sea was a common activity in the time of Hesiod.

Certainly, Askra could have been immune from these developments and from knowledge of seafaring. Hesiod, however, talks of small and large ships. He advises on proper storage of the ship during inclement weather: drag it onto dry land, surround it with stones, pull out the bilge plug,

---

54. Personal conversation together with information from their sailing diary.

The harbor of Kreusis, outlet to the Corinthian Gulf. (Photograph by Richard R. Johnson and used with his permission)

store the equipment carefully, and hang the steering oar in the smoke of the hearth (45, 624–29). Moreover, the evidence of geography reveals that Askra is not out of touch with the sea. Askra is within the sphere of Thespiai, which is given as the seaport of Kreusis on the Corinthian Gulf by later sources (Pausanias 9.21.1; Strabo 9.2.25). Some seven to eight kilometers (five miles) separate Askra from Thespiai, whereas Kreusis is about thirty kilometers (about twenty miles) distant from Thespiai. Archaeologists have uncovered an old stone road between Thespiai and Kreusis. It has been estimated that a "traveler from Ascra could reach the port in a single day, moving at a speed of 3 kilometers per hour (ox limit)."[55] There is another possible shipping place for the region on the Dombraian Gulf, south of Thisbe, slightly more distant than Kreusis but still within one or two days' walk from Askra.

55. W. K. Pritchett, *Studies in Ancient Greek Topography,* 54; R. J. Buck, *A History of Boeotia,* iv, map 2 cited by Tandy, *Warriors into Traders,* 213–14 (quotation on 213).

In sum, *Works and Days* reports that the poet's father had taken to the sea in search of a better life and had found his way to Askra. The poet himself had journeyed to the eastern coast of Boeotia—not a difficult trek—in order to cross the water to Euboea. And he tries to turn his brother's thoughts from trade (*emporia*). It is true that Hesiod is not enthusiastic about seafaring, but perhaps his caution is further indication that he belongs to a particular time and place in Greek history: a time when travel by sea was recently under way and a place somewhat removed from direct access to the sea. If we do not take recourse in striking all these references to seafaring, the poem accords nicely with conditions evident in Greece during the time when Hesiod is generally thought to have lived.

Literary criticism adds another support to the significance of the sea in Hesiod's age. In her recent study *The Raft of Odysseus,* Carol Dougherty details the relationship between the epics and their eighth-century context. That the sea is a central image of the *Odyssey* hardly needs mention: it defines Odysseus's ten-year return from Troy, describes the people he encounters, and informs his tales. In addition, the epic mirrors the world of archaic Greece. Odysseus, as Dougherty concludes, is a "new hero for a new age. . . . [I]nstead of a hero who stands and fights to the death to defend his established way of life, Odysseus represents the potential of travel—both its opportunities and its risks. He helps open up the world across the sea to those Greeks at home."[56]

Opportunities are at the same time risks. Would-be colonizers may happen upon the Phaeacians who offer guest friendship, or they may encounter the cannibalistic Cyclopes. The two quite different encounters convey the "two ways Greeks experience new peoples in the New World." Would-be traders may meet the piratical Phoenicians, or they may deal with Mentes who engages in a reciprocal form of exchange and, at the same time, stands within the protection of aristocratic guest friendship and gift exchange. The problematic nature of these polarities is reflected in the epic: "The *Odyssey* imagines a place for Greeks overseas, it speculates about new means of exchange and value, and above all, it celebrates the power and potential of narrative to articulate these new ways of life in a world of upheaval and change."[57]

---

56. Dougherty, *The Raft of Odysseus,* 176.
57. Ibid., 103, 47–48, 175.

Hesiod mentions both activities enabled by the sea: travel and trade. He is proof of the kind of concern that would have been felt in a world of sudden change. And it is not surprising that his advice is somewhat contradictory; he instructs Perses on seafaring and trading, even though Hesiod knows that people of the golden age did not travel on ships. They had no need to tempt Poseidon's wrath since the earth bore the produce they needed (236–37). Moreover, Hesiod is angry over the causes making the new, inferior way of life necessary. Recent developments have, in David Tandy's words, "wreaked havoc."[58] One of the main causes is the increasing difficulty of filling barns with sustenance (307).

Some of the fault lies with the land of Greece, which is not a friend to farmers. Three-quarters of Greece is mountainous, much of the soil is thin, rainfall is extremely limited in parts of the country, and, throughout the country, very little rain falls during the summer and early autumn months. The rain that does occur takes the form of torrential storms that are more damaging to crops than nourishing. In a word, "much of the Greek countryside is marginal for arable agriculture."[59] Most Greek farmers would understand Hesiod's advice to work, then work harder, even when no exceptional calamities occur. "Work is no disgrace, idleness is!" (311).

However, the eighth century produced new challenges and new opportunities. It is estimated that ten thousand people left Greece to settle in colonies before 700.[60] The vitality of Greek culture from its beginnings to the present day can be read on the barometer of seafaring. Internal vitality reflects itself in active command of the sea, whereas periods of decline are regularly accompanied by retreat from the sea. In the eighth century, Greeks are returning to their sailing vessels, some with enthusiasm, others reluctantly.

Another concern of some critics is the references to the dispute (neikos) between Hesiod and Perses. There were hard feelings over the original inheritance, and now Hesiod seeks a final proper solution between the brothers without interference from the gift-devouring lords. Some readers of Hesiod's poems—many of whom are ardent admirers of those poems—

58. Tandy, Warriors into Traders, 83.
59. Osborne, Classical Landscape with Figures, 31.
60. Morris, Archaeology and Cultural History, 257.

conclude that the quarrel, like Perses himself, is literary fiction.[61] Even people who accept Hesiod and Perses as historical figures question details of the dispute. For others, the picture of lords judging disputes in an agora in Askra is impossible. "Where are we, anyway, Askra or Athens?"[62]

Size—either of population or community extent—does not an agora make. The *Odyssey* indicates the presence of agoras in Pylos (3.31), Phaeacia (6.266–67, 8.16), and Ithaka (17.52). And in the *Iliad* the temporary camp of the Achaeans at Troy boasts an agora in the middle of the ships (8.220) with seats for judges who will administer justice (11.806–8), and the dispute described on Achilles' shield takes place in an agora (18.497). Archaeological evidence reveals that even the little polis of Dreros on Crete had an agora, the oldest known example dating to the eighth century. The function of an agora, both in the epic picture and in the concrete world of archaeological evidence, was to serve as the public space. That one use of this space was the adjudication of quarrels is evident in the location of the early codes of law, namely, as inscriptions on temple walls— another symbol of the collective nature of community.[63] The temples, especially in the eighth and seventh centuries, are not remote and isolated from the polis centers but, rather, lie at the heart of the public space.

Moreover, as we have seen, a hatred of strife and a corresponding concern with straight justice pervades Hesiodic poetry: the two kinds of Strife described in line 11 of *Works and Days* appear also in *Theogony* (226–32). One of the notable characteristics of abhorrent Strife is that she causes quarrels, falsehoods, disputes, and faulty law. A general concern with justice accords well with the economic changes associated with private ownership of property and goods. Developments affecting land use and leading to a concentration of land in the hands of fewer owners have provoked conflict through history. The poet of *Works and Days* tells us that such changes had impacted people in Askra: Perses is in debt (405, 647), and he is begging from others (399–402). Apparently, he must make a new

---

61. Gilbert Murray made such an assertion in 1897 in *A History of Ancient Greek Literature*, 6–7, 53–55; more recently, this was the conclusion of Fritz Krafft, *Vergleichende Untersuchungen zu Homer und Hesiod*, 90.

62. Lamberton, *Hesiod*, 114.

63. See Karl Joachim Hölkeskamp, "*Agorai* bei Homer" and "Tempel, Agora, und Alphabet: Die Entstehungsbedingungen von Gesetzbegung in der archaischen Polis."

start—"get a house, a slave woman, and an ox for the plough" (405–6)—
and Hesiod tells him how to build the plow (427–36). This personal experience with strife and its inadequate solution may well have been the
motivation for the composition of the poem.

Peter Green has made an interesting argument that lines 1 through 285
express "a dramatic commemoration of a personal experience." Although
this interpretation entails reinterpretation of certain of the specific references to the lawsuit and the nature of the quarrel, it clearly preserves a
concern for proper justice in Hesiod's poetry and the real world. If Hesiod
did re-create his plea after the event, as Green proposes, the reality of that
event is not in doubt: "[T]he details are too circumstantial, too idiosyn-
cratic, too involved to suggest—especially ca. 700 B.C.—a sophisticated
fiction masquerading as truth."[64]

Is this a singer-writer who "establishes an ironic distance from his persona," as Lamberton asks, and, we might add, from the world he claims as
his own?[65] Or does a coherent personality emerge from the poems?

A man who names himself "Hesiod" and claims to be a farmer in Askra
reveals an identity through his injunctions. He is not a happy man: "Would
that I had not been born of the fifth generation of mortals but had died
earlier or been born later for now is a race of iron" (174–76). Mortal life is
constant, backbreaking work. And an honest man must beware the snares
set by many, even a brother or a wife. A great deal of his wrath fastens
upon wrongdoers, especially that group of lords who pass crooked judgments, not fearing the gods' wrath (250–51). But even arrogant men are
watched by all-seeing Zeus (238–39), nor is it possible to deceive or out-
wit the mind of Zeus (*Theogony* 613–14). The poet's faith in the power of
the gods is unshaken. *Works and Days* begins with a call to the Muses to
chant the praise of their father, Zeus, and its close enjoins us to watch
carefully the days that come from Zeus. In addition to this cosmic knowledge that Zeus is watchful of proper behavior, Hesiod notes that even
daily life can bring some pleasant surprises: drinking bibline wine in the
shade during the hot summer (588–96), inviting a friend to a feast (342),
finding a good wife (702), or winning a contest in song (655–59). A voice,

64. Green, "Works and Days 1–285," 39, 49.
65. Lamberton, *Hesiod,* 150.

a unified voice, emerges from the poetry. No similar voice finds expression in the *Iliad* and *Odyssey*. But it speaks strongly in the poems of Archilochus (ca. 680–640 BCE): "I am two things," "I do not like," "I will make nothing better by crying," "If it only were my fortune just to touch Neoboule's hand" (trans. Lattimore, *Greek Lyrics*). We remember that Hesiod's poems have been dated to 700–650 BCE.

Conclusion

Shall we conclude that Hesiod is best viewed as a name of all those bards and rhapsodists who sang traditional verses from the nonliterate days of the Dark Age to the literate times of the Hellenistic world? Such a conclusion is feasible only by dismissing:

1. all personal references to people and places;

2. the actuality of events such as funeral games in honor of Amphidamas of Chalkis, associated with a conflict between two poleis dated to around 700 BCE;

3. the instructions on farming as representing necessary information;

4. the possibility of earning a livelihood through trade by sea as well as by farming;

5. anger over unfair division of property as a sign of pressure on the land evident in the large-scale colonization movement beginning about 750;

6. dislike and distrust of gift-devouring lords as indicative of actual political and economic power by the end of the eighth century;

7. signs that an individual's well-being was dependent upon proper collective behavior;

8. the association of *Theogony* and *Works and Days* with the Homeric epics on the grounds of common characteristics but dated later than those epics on stylistic grounds;

9. a perception of a coherent personality and voice in the poetry; and

10. the possibility that Hesiod was literate.

A dismissal is all the more difficult in that these features of the poems attributed to a person named Hesiod fit so closely both with one another and into the period of the late eighth and early seventh centuries, the period to which "Hesiod" is dated on grounds of the nature of his poetry. David Tandy has suggested "that Hesiod, poet of *Works and Days*, is better discerned less as an individual than as a representative . . . of the individual members of the particular class of politically and economically excluded persons."[66] Surely, he is both a representative and a specific individual, for when a handful of lords is dominant, most people will be members of that excluded class. Hesiod tells us that he belongs to that class. We happen to be fortunate in having the view of one of those people, whose name was Hesiod.

66. Tandy, *Warriors into Traders*, 13.

Afterword

I have sought to recover the identity of actual individuals within pre-classical Greece following the stories of a hero often associated with myth or legend and a poet some would describe as a fictitious construct of every poet who composed didactic verse. Why is this a worthwhile endeavor?

First, the primary goal of history is the recovery and recounting of the human story. And, second, at the heart of this story are real people rather than constructed categories. A third factor relates to challenges to traditional history: since the mid-twentieth century, several points of disagreement with earlier approaches to understanding the human past have emerged. Some would deny that the intentions, motivations, and values of actors in the past can be recovered. Human-related disciplines have adopted new tools, statistical methods, and theoretical approaches that pushed people into the background, while postmodern beliefs eliminate knowledge of humans and objects associated with them. In the words of Michel Foucault, "[T]o all those who wish to take [man] as their 'starting-point' in their attempts to reach the truth . . . we can answer only with a philosophical laugh—which means, to a certain extent a silent one."[1]

The figures of Jason, a warrior from the age of heroes, and Hesiod, a farmer-poet who lived in the late eighth and early seventh centuries, are good examples to test all three propositions. Through them, we can learn whether the limited evidence from preclassical Greece is sufficient to reveal the human story through individuals. If so, we can then ask how Jason and Hesiod open new windows into their worlds. If the evidence

1. Foucault, *Order of Things,* 342–43.

has been sufficient and new insights have been given, we will find that the extreme positions of the "new" human-related disciplines and of post-modernism have not prevailed to produce "history without people."[2]

The means of examining the historical reality of the two people followed the same procedure, namely, drawing on every available category of evidence. The evidence was similar but varied in accord with the specific nature of evidence for each period, separated as they are by seven or eight hundred years.

To learn more about Jason, archaeological evidence has carried more weight than textual data, since Linear B records are limited in number, in locations where they have been found, and through their purpose as administrative records of goods, places, animals, and personnel. By contrast, in Hesiod's time alphabetic writing was in use in the Greek world, at least in the form of brief inscriptions. But from this beginning, the script would expand to preserve epic tales, to codify laws, and even to recount personal concerns. Hesiod himself seems to have possessed the skill of writing, using it for two poems regularly attributed to him. Due to these differences, Hesiod describes his circumstances, including reactions to them, whereas Jason is mute. Yet the Linear B records provide important clues: the syllabary is adapted to the Greek language, and it was essential as a product of centralized administrative structures. Consequently, we can add a known language and a social, political context to a portrait of Jason. Moreover, specific words may well include the name *i-wa-so* (a Mycenaean form of *Jason*) and *ko-ki-do* (or *Colchis,* by Mycenaean spelling rules).

Archaeology has demonstrated the reality of citadel centers whose rulers directed the affairs of fairly extensive regions in the Bronze Age. Some of the earliest finds were in southern Greece. Just recently, important discoveries show that a location near modern Volos is likely to be a northern center remembered as Iolkos. Thus, we have a fixed location. Objects uncovered in the area show a degree of wealth comparable to that of, say, Mycenae. Survey archaeology presents a picture of a productive agrarian economy in the region, while scientific analysis of pottery reveals direct links with other parts of Greece. That inhabitants of Iolkos participated in seafaring for trade, or other, purposes is suggested by the fine

2. From the title of an article by Le Roy Ladurie, "History without People."

harbor at Volos, a fondness for pictures of ships, and the lively tempo of Aegean sea travel in the Bronze Age. Penetration into the Black Sea in the second millennium has been documented by the construction of a modern *Argo,* using Bronze Age technology, which was successfully taken through the difficult Bosporus strait to the eastern end of the Black Sea. At its destination, by the way, gold was trapped in sheepskins pegged on boards and sunk in streambeds.

Excavation has not uncovered Askra, something that is not surprising since Hesiod's description indicates that it was a hamlet, certainly not a regional center or even a considerable village. But the use of survey archaeology has demonstrated the existence of a small settlement in a location that corresponds with natural features mentioned in *Works and Days* and *Theogony.* Examination of the larger region of Boeotia provides a likely port on the Gulf of Corinth and a location on the Euboean straits whence a man from Askra would set sail to compete in song in funeral games at the Euboean town of Chalkis.

A third source of information is now better understood: oral transmission of information and entertainment can stretch over many generations. Literacy was limited in the Bronze Age, but oral poetry—poetized speech—can fill needs other than administrative accountancy. Beyond a belief that accounts and songs composed and remembered by oral transmission must have existed, similarities exist between the form of Greek on the tablets and that of Homeric Greek. Additionally, there are links in archaeological finds from the Mycenaean age and objects described in the *Iliad* and *Odyssey.* Thus, a tale of events in the Bronze Age sung by an eighth-century bard may well have had roots in the Mycenaean era. It is unlikely to have been preserved in writing, since Linear B seems to have vanished with the collapse of the Bronze Age citadel centers. The art of writing was recovered, albeit in a new form, only four centuries after that collapse. Appreciation of the twin skills of a poet living around 700 BCE—namely, oral composition based on an inherited tradition and the new skill of writing—fits well the form and nature of the two poems attributed to Hesiod.

For both periods it is possible to reconstruct the nature of life for people then living. Alliances between history and other disciplines examining the human story in various ways allow an understanding of use of land and its changes over time, means of subsistence, the organization of society, the physical characteristics of humans, and the nonbiological traits of their cultures. Incorporation of specialized scientific technology such as analysis of DNA has refined the interpretation of clues left behind by earlier humans.

Use of all these approaches to the past shows a consistency between accounts preserved orally, or largely so, and the picture that emerges from the human-related disciplines. As a result, we have an image of the Bronze Age circumstances of the "hero" Jason and another of the early-seventh-century nonelite farmer-poet Hesiod.

Why is this valuable?

First, I would conclude that even the limited evidence for Mycenaean Greece and the age of revolution can reveal the human story in the form of named individuals. These individuals provide insights that speak across the millennia to people of the twenty-first century in ways that categories of people cannot. Just as people of the past used Jason and Hesiod to understand their world, so too we must understand their reality to comprehend the history of preclassical Greece. Finally, the results indicate that the "new" human-related disciplines and postmodern approaches have not won the contest over the true subject of history in any period of history, including preclassical Greece.

Bibliography

Ammerman, Albert J., and L. L. Cavalli-Sforza. *The Neolithic Transition and the Genetics of Populations in Europe.* Princeton: Princeton University Press, 1984.

Andreou, Stelios, Michael Fotiadis, and Kostas Kotsakis. "Aegean Prehistory V: The Neolithic and Bronze Age of Northern Greece." In *Aegean Prehistory: A Review, Archaeology,* ed. Tracey Cullen, supp. 1, 537–97. Boston: Archaeological Institute of America, 2001.

Artzy, M. "Routes, Trade, Boats, and 'Nomads of the Sea.'" In *Mediterranean Peoples in Transition, Thirteenth to Early Tenth Centuries BCE,* ed. S. Gitin, A. Mazar, and E. Stern, 444–45. Jerusalem: Israel Exploration Society, 1998.

Bapty, I. "Nietzsche, Derrida, Foucault: ReExcavating the Meaning of Archaeology." In *Archaeology after Structuralism: Post-structuralism and the Problem of Archaeology,* ed. I. Bapty and I. Yates, 240–76. New York: Routledge, 1990.

Barber, R. L. N. "The Mycenaeans and the Cyclades." In *The Cyclades in the Bronze Age,* 224–36. Iowa City: University of Iowa Press, 1987.

Bass, G. F., C. Pulak, D. Collon, and J. Weinstein. "The Bronze Age Shipwreck at Ulu Burun: 1986 Campaign." *American Journal of Archaeology* 93 (1989): 1–29.

Bassett, Samuel. *The Poetry of Homer.* Berkeley and Los Angeles: University of California Press, 1938.

Behr, H.-J., G. Biegel, and H. Castritius, eds. *Traum und Wirklichkeit: Troia: Ein Mythos in Geschichte und Rezeption.* Sumposion im Braunschweigischen Landesmuseum am 8. und 9. June 2001. Brauschweig: Theiss, 2002.

Bentley, Michael. "Stones from the Glasshouse." *Times Literary Supplement* (August 30, 2002): 10–11.

Berelov, Ilya. "Metamythics: The Epistemological Problems of Archaeology." *Helios* 23:1 (1996): 90–104.

Berlin, Isaiah. "The Concept of Scientific History." In *Concepts and Categories: Philosophical Essays,* ed. H. Hardy, 103–42. New York: Hogarth Press, 1978.

Binford, Lewis R. *In Pursuit of the Past: Decoding the Archaeological Record.* New York: Thames and Hudson, 1983.

———. "The 'New Archaeology,' Then and Now." In *Archaeological Thought in America,* ed. C. C. Lamberg-Karlovsky, 50–62. Cambridge: Cambridge University Press, 1989.

Binford, Sally R., and Lewis R. Binford, eds. *New Perspectives in Archaeology.* Chicago: Aldine Publishing, 1968.

Bintliff, John. "Reflections on Nine Years with the Bradford-Cambridge Boeotia Project." *Boiotika Antiqua* 8 (1989): 13–21.

———. "A Review of Contemporary Perspectives on the 'Meaning' of the Past." In *Extracting Meaning from the Past,* ed. John Bintliff, 3–36. Oxford: Oxbow Books, 1988.

Bintliff, John, and Kostas Sbonias, eds. *Reconstructing Past Population Trends in Mediterranean Europe (3000 BC–AD 1800).* Oxford: Oxbow Books, 1999.

Bottéro, J., C. Herrenschmidt, and J.-P. Vernant. *Ancestor of the West: Writing, Reasoning, and Religion in Mesopotamia, Elam, and Greece.* Chicago: University of Chicago Press, 2000.

Bouzek, Jan. *Greece, Anatolia, and Europe: Cultural Interrelations during the Early Iron Age.* Jonsered: Paul Åströms Förlag, 1997.

Bower, Bruce. "The Brain in the Machine: Biologically Inspired Computer Models Renew Debates over the Nature of Thought." *Science News* 134 (November 26, 1988): 344–45.

Bowersock, G. W., and T. J. Cornell, eds. *Studies on Modern Scholarship.* Berkeley and Los Angeles: University of California Press, 1994.

Bradbury, Malcolm. *My Strange Quest for Mensonge.* London: André Deutsch, 1987.

Braudel, Fernand. "History and Sociology." In *On History,* trans. Sarah Matthews, 64–82. Chicago: University of Chicago Press, 1980.

———. "History and the Social Sciences: The Longue Durée." In *On History*, trans. Sarah Matthews, 25–54. Chicago: University of Chicago Press, 1980.

———. "Is There a Geography of Biological Man?" In *On History*, trans. Sarah Matthews, 105–19. Chicago: University of Chicago Press, 1980.

———. "The Situation in History in 1950." In *On History*, trans. Sarah Matthews, 6–22. Chicago: University of Chicago Press, 1980.

Brilliant, Richard. *My Laocoon: Alternative Claims in the Interpretation of Artworks*. Berkeley and Los Angeles: University of California Press, 2000.

Buck, R. J. *A History of Boeotia*. Alberta: University of Alberta Press, 1979.

Butrica, L. Review of *Propertius: Modernist Poet of Antiquity*, by D. Thomas Benediktson. *Classical Review* (1990): 266–68.

Cannadine, David. "What Is History Today?" *Historically Speaking* (February 2003): 4–6.

———, ed. *What Is History Now?* New York: Palgrave Macmillan, 2002.

Carpenter, Rhys. "The Greek Penetration of the Black Sea." *American Journal of Archaeology* 52 (1948): 1–10.

Carr, E. H. *What Is History?* London: Macmillan, 1961.

Catling, H. W., and A. Millett. "A Study of the Inscribed Stirrup-Jars from Thebes." *Archaeometry* 8 (1965): 3–85.

Chadwick, John. "Mycenaean Elements in the Homeric Dialect." *Minoica* 12 (1958): 116–22.

Clare, R. J. "Epic Itineraries: The Sea and Seafaring in the *Odyssey* of Homer and the *Argonautica* of Apollonius Rhodius." In *The Sea in Antiquity*, ed. G. J. Oliver, R. Brock, T. J. Cornell, and S. Hodkinson, 1–12. BAR International Series 899. Oxford: Hadrian Books, 2000.

Clarke, David. *Analytical Archaeology*. London: Methuen, 1968.

Cline, Eric H. *Sailing the Wine-Dark Sea: International Trade in the Late Bronze Age Aegean*. Oxford: Tempus Reparatum, 1994.

Cline, Eric H., and Diane Harris-Cline, eds. *The Aegean and the Orient in the Second Millennium*. Aegaeum 18. Liège: University of Liège, 1998.

Davies, Anna Morpurgo. "Personal Names and Linguistic Continuity." In *Greek Personal Names: Their Value as Evidence*, ed. Simon Hornblower and Elaine Mathews, 15–39. Proceedings of the British Academy, vol. 104. Oxford: Oxford University Press, 2000.

Davies, John. "Greek History: A Discipline in Transformation." In *Classics in Progress: Essays on Ancient Greece and Rome,* ed. T. P. Wiseman, 225–46. Oxford: Oxford University Press, 2002.

Davison, J. A. *Companion to Homer.* London: Macmillan, 1962.

Deetz, James. *Invitation to Archaeology.* New York: Natural History Press, 1967.

Detienne, Marcel. *The Creation of Mythology.* Trans. Margaret Cook. Chicago: University of Chicago Press, 1986. Originally published as *L'invention de la mythologie.* Paris: Éditions Gallinard, 1981.

Donald, Merlin. *A Mind So Rare.* New York: W. W. Norton, 2001.

Donlan, Walter. "The Pre-state Community in Greece." *Symbolae Osloenses* 64 (1989): 5–29.

———. "The Relations of Power in the Pre-state and Early State Politics." In *The Development of the Polis in Archaic Greece,* ed. L. G. Mitchell and P. J. Rhodes, 39–48. London: Routledge, 1997.

Dougherty, Carol. *The Raft of Odysseus.* Oxford: Oxford University Press, 2001.

Dow, Sterling. "Literacy: The Palace Bureaucracies, the Dark Age, Homer." In *A Land Called Crete,* 109–47. Northampton, MA: Smith College, 1968.

Edwards, G. P. *The Language of Hesiod in Its Traditional Context.* Oxford: Basil Blackwell, 1971.

Encyclopedia of the Social Sciences. New York: Macmillan, 1937.

Eriksson, Sven A., and Paul Åström. *Fingerprints and Archaeology.* Studies in Mediterranean Archaeology 28. Göteborg, Sweden: P. Åström, 1980.

Evans, Richard J. *In Defence of History.* London: Granta Books, 1997.

Evelyn-White, Hugh G., trans. *Hesiod: The Homeric Hymns and Homerica.* London: Wm. Heinemann, 1982.

Finley, Moses I. *The World of Odysseus.* Rev. ed. 1954. Reprint, New York: Viking Press, 1978.

Foucault, Michel. *The Order of Things: An Archaeology of the Human Sciences.* 1960 (original French publication). Reprint, New York: Pantheon Books.

Fox, Robin Lane. "Hellenistic Culture and Literature." In *The Oxford History of the Classical World,* ed. J. Boardman, J. Griffin, and O. Murray, 338–64. Oxford: Oxford University Press, 1986.

Fox-Genovese, E., and E. Lasch-Quinn, eds. *Reconstructing History: The Emergence of a New Historical Society.* New York: Routledge, 1999.

Frazer, P. M., and E. Matthews, eds. *Lexicon of Greek Personal Names IIIB:*

Central Greece from the Megarid to Thessaly. Oxford: Clarendon Press, 2000.

Frost, Frank. Review of *Who Killed Homer? The Decline of Classical Education and the Recovery of Greek Wisdom,* by Victor Davis Hanson and John Heath. *New England Classical Journal* 26:3 (1999): 44–46.

Furet, François. "Quantitative History." In *Historical Studies Today,* ed. F. Gilbert and S. Graubard, 45–61. New York: W. W. Norton, 1972.

Gagarin, Michael. *Early Greek Law.* Berkeley and Los Angeles: University of California Press, 1986.

Geertz, Clifford. *Works and Lives: The Anthropologist as Author.* Stanford: Stanford University Press, 1988.

Gellner, Ernest. "What Is Structuralisme?" In *Theory and Explanation in Archaeology,* ed. C. Renfrew, M. H. Rowlands, and B. A. Segraves, 97–123. New York: Academic Press, 1982.

Graf, Fritz. "Medea, the Enchantress from Afar: Remarks on a Well-Known Myth." In *Medea: Essays on Medea in Myth, Literature, Philosophy, and Art,* ed. J. J. Clauss and S. I. Johnston, 21–43. Princeton: Princeton University Press, 1997.

Graham, A. J. "The Date of the Greek Penetration of the Black Sea." *Bulletin of the Institute of Classical Studies* 5 (1958): 25–42.

Green, Peter. *Alexander to Actium: The Historical Evolution of the Hellenistic Age.* Berkeley and Los Angeles: University of California Press, 1990.

———. "Works and Days 1–285: Hesiod's Invisible Audience." In *Mnemai: Classical Studies in Memory of Karl K. Hulley,* ed. Harold D. Evjen, 21–39. Chico, CA: Scholars Press, 1984.

Gregory, Elizabeth. "Unraveling Penelope: The Construction of the Faithful Wife in Homer's Heroines." *Helios* 23:1 (1996): 3–20.

Habakkuk, John. "Economic History and Economic Theory." In *Historical Studies Today,* ed. F. Gilbert and S. Graubard, 27–44. New York: W. W. Norton, 1972.

Halliburton, D. "Concealing Revealing: A Perspective on Greek Tragedy." In *Post-structuralist Classics,* ed. A. Benjamin, 245–67. New York: Routledge, 1988.

Hamilton, Edith. *Mythology.* New York: Mentor Books, 1953.

Hamilton, Richard. *The Architecture of Hesiod's Poetry.* Baltimore: Johns Hopkins University Press, 1989.

Hampe, Roland, and Erika Simon. *The Birth of Greek Art: From the*

Mycenaean to the Archaic Period. New York: Oxford University Press, 1981.

Hanson, Victor Davis, and John Heath. *Who Killed Homer? The Decline of Classical Education and the Recovery of Greek Wisdom.* New York: Free Press, 1998.

Hartog, François. *Memories of Odysseus: Frontier Tales from Ancient Greece.* Trans. J. Lloyd. Chicago: University of Chicago Press, 2001.

Havelock, Eric A. "The Greek Alphabet." In *The Literate Revolution in Greece and Its Cultural Consequences,* 77–88. Princeton: Princeton University Press, 1982.

————. "The Transcription of the Code of a Non-literate Culture." In *The Literate Revolution in Greece and Its Cultural Consequences,* 89–121. Princeton: Princeton University Press, 1982.

Hawkes, Jacquetta. *Nothing But or Something More.* Seattle: University of Washington Press, 1972.

————. "The Proper Study of Mankind." *Antiquity* 42 (1968): 255–62.

Heimlich, Rüdiger. "The New Trojan Wars." *Archaeology Odyssey* (July–August 2002): 16–23.

Heubeck, A. "L'origine della lineare B." *Studi micenei ed egeo-anatolici* 23 (1982): 195–217.

Hillar, Stephan. "The Mycenaeans and the Black Sea." *Thalassa: L'Egee Prehistorique et la Mer. Aegaeum* 7 (1991): 207–16.

Himmelfarb, Gertrude. "Clio and the New History." In *The New History and the Old,* 33–46. Cambridge: Harvard University Press, Belknap Press, 1987.

————. "History with the Politics Left Out." In *The New History and the Old,* 13–32. Cambridge: Harvard University Press, Belknap Press, 1987.

————. "Postmodernist History." Reprinted in *Reconstructing History: The Emergence of a New Historical Society,* ed. E. Fox-Genovese and E. Lasch-Quinn, 71–93. New York: Routledge, 1999. Originally published in *On Looking into the Abyss.* New York: Alfred A. Knopf, 1994.

————. "Two Nations or Five Classes." In *The New History and the Old,* 47–69. Cambridge: Harvard University Press, Belknap Press, 1987.

Hölkeskamp, Karl Joachim. "*Agorai* bei Homer." In *Volk und Verfassung im vorhellenistischen Griechenland,* ed. W. Eder and Karl Joachim Hölkeskamp, 1–19. Stuttgart: Franz Steiner, 1997.

————. "Tempel, Agora, und Alphabet: Die Entstehungsbedingungen von Gesetzbegung in der archaischen Polis." In *Rechtskodifizierung und soziale Normen im interkulturellen Vergleich,* ed. Han-Joachim Gehrke, 135–64. Tübingen: Gunter Narr Verlag, 1994.

Hooker, James T. *Mycenaean Greece.* London: Routledge and Kegan Paul, 1976.

Hornblower, Simon, and Elaine Matthews, eds. *Greek Personal Names: Their Value as Evidence,* 15–39. Proceedings of the British Academy, vol. 104. Oxford: Oxford University Press, 2000.

Hudson, Pat. *Encyclopedia of Historians and Historical Writing.* Chicago: Fitzroy Dearborn Publications, 1999.

Hunt, Lynn. "President's Report." *Perspectives* (newsmagazine of the American Historical Association) (May 2002): 7–9.

Huppert, George. "President's Corner." *Historically Speaking* (May 2001): 3.

Immerwahr, Sara A. "Some Pictorial Fragments from Iolkos." *Archaiologike Efemeris* (1985): 85–94.

Jacoby, F. *Die Fragmente der Griechischen Historiker.* 1927. Reprint, Leiden: Brill, 1957–1969.

Janko, Richard. *Homer, Hesiod, and the Hymns: Diachronic Development in Epic Diction.* Cambridge: Cambridge University Press, 1982.

Jaynes, Julian. *The Origin of Consciousness in the Breakdown of the Bicameral Mind.* Boston: Houghton Mifflin, 1976.

Jeffery, L. *Archaic Greece: The City States c. 700–500 B.C.* London: Ernest Benn, 1976.

Kahane, Ahuvia. *The Interpretation of Order: A Study in the Poetics of Homeric Repetition.* Oxford: Clarendon Press, 1994.

Kearsley, R. A. "Greeks Overseas in the 8th Century B.C." In *Ancient Greeks West and East,* ed. G. R. Tsetskhladze, 109–34. Leiden: Brill, 1999.

Killebrew, A. "Mycenaean and Aegean-Type Pottery in Canaan during the 14th–12th Centuries BC." In *The Aegean and the Orient in the Second Millennium,* ed. Eric H. Cline and Diane Harris-Cline, 159–66. *Aegaeum* 18. Liège: University of Liège, 1998.

Kirk, Geoffrey. *Myth: Its Meaning and Functions in Ancient and Other Cultures.* Berkeley and Los Angeles: University of California Press, 1970.

Korfmann, M. "An Ancient Anatolian Palatial and Trading Center:

Archaeological Evidence for the Period of Troia VI/VII." In *The World of Troy: Homer, Schliemann, and the Treasures of Priam*, 15–74. Washington, DC: Society for the Preservation of the Greek Heritage, 1997.

———. "Troy: Topography and Navigation." In *Troy and the Trojan War: A Symposium Held at Bryn Mawr College, October 1984*, 1–16. Bryn Mawr, PA: Bryn Mawr College, 1986.

Krafft, Fritz. *Vergleichende Untersuchungen zu Homer und Hesiod*. Göttingen: Vandenhoeck and Ruprecht, 1963.

Kraft, J. C. "Geology and Paleogeographic Reconstructions of the Vicinity of Troy." In *Troy: The Archeological Geology*, ed. G. Rapp and J. A. Gifford, supp. monograph 4, 11–41. Princeton: Princeton University Press, 1982.

Kraft, J. C., I. Kayan, and O. Erol. "Geomorphic Reconstructions in the Environs of Ancient Troy." *Science* 209 (August 15, 1980): 776–82.

Kretschmer, P. "Mythische Namen." *Glotta* 10 (1920): 38–61.

Labaree, Benjamin. "How the Greeks Sailed into the Black Sea." *American Journal of Archaeology* 61 (1957): 29–33.

Lamberton, Robert. *Hesiod*. New Haven: Yale University Press, 1988.

Lateiner, Donald. Review of *Epitheta Hominum apud Homerum*, by James H. Dee. *Bryn Mawr Classical Review* (January 1, 2001).

Lattimore, Richmond, trans. *Hesiod*. Ann Arbor: University of Michigan Press, 1959.

Leaf, Walter. *Troy: A Study in Homeric Geography*. London: Macmillan, 1912.

Le Roy Ladurie, Emmanuel. *The Territory of the Historian*. Trans. Siân Reynolds and Ben Reynolds. Chicago: University of Chicago Press, 1979.

Levi, Peter. *The Pelican History of Greek Literature*. Harmondsworth: Penguin Books, 1985.

Lodge, David. *Thinks*. New York: Viking, 2001.

Lord, Albert B. "Characteristics of Orality." *Oral Tradition* 2:1 (1987): 54–72.

Luce, J. V. *Celebrating Homer's Landscapes: Troy and Ithaca Revisited*. New Haven: Yale University Press, 1998.

Lyttkens, C. H. "The Origins of the Polis: An Economic Perspective on Institutional Change in Ancient Greece, 1000–600 B.C." Not yet published; sent to author for comment.

MacMullen, Ramsay. *Feelings in History.* Claremont, CA: Regina Books, 2003.

Manning, Stuart. "From Process to People: Longue Durée to History." In *The Aegean and the Orient in the Second Millennium,* ed. Eric H. Cline and Diane Harris-Cline, 311–25. *Aegaeum* 18. Liège: University of Liège, 1998.

McDonald, William A., and George R. Rapp Jr. *The Minnesota Messenia Expedition: Reconstructing a Bronze Age Regional Environment.* Minneapolis: University of Minnesota Press, 1972.

McNeill, William H. *A World History.* 2d ed. Oxford: Oxford University Press, 1967.

Mee, C. "Anatolia and the Aegean in the Late Bronze Age." In *The Aegean and the Orient in the Second Millennium,* ed. Eric H. Cline and Diane Harris-Cline, 137–45. *Aegaeum* 18. Liège: University of Liège, 1998.

Merrilles, R. "Egypt and the Aegean." In *The Aegean and the Orient in the Second Millennium,* ed. Eric H. Cline and Diane Harris-Cline, 149–54. *Aegaeum* 18. Liège: University of Liège, 1998.

Mitchell, G., and P. J. Rhodes, eds. *The Development of the Polis in Archaic Greece.* London: Routledge, 1997.

Mitchell, S. "Archaeology in Asia Minor, 1979–84." *Archaeological Reports* (1984–1985): 70–105.

Morell, K. Scott. "Chaos Theory and the Oral Tradition: Nonlinearity and Bifurcation in the *Iliad.*" *Helios* 23:2 (Fall 1996): 107–34.

Morris, Ian. *Archaeology and Cultural History: Words and Things in Iron Age Greece.* Oxford: Blackwell, 2000.

Morrison, J. S., and R. T. Williams. *Greek Oared Ships, 900–322 BC.* Cambridge: Cambridge University Press, 1968.

Muhly, James. "Gold Analysis and Sources of Gold in the Bronze Age." *Temple University Aegean Symposium* 8 (1983): 1–14.

Mure, William. *A Critical History of the Language and Literature of Ancient Greece.* Vol. 2. London, 1854.

Murray, Gilbert. *A History of Ancient Greek Literature.* London, 1897.

Murray, William. "Ancient Sailing Winds in the Eastern Mediterranean: The Case for Cyprus." In *Proceedings of the International Symposium Cyprus and the Sea,* ed. Vassos Karageorghis and Demetrios Michaelides, 33–44. Nicosia: University of Cyprus, 1995.

————. "Do Modern Winds Equal Ancient Winds?" *Mediterranean Historical Review* 2:2 (1987): 139–67.

Musgrave, J. H., R. A. H. Neave, and A. J. N. W. Prag. "Seven Faces from Grave Circle B at Mycenae." *Annual of the British School at Athens* 90 (1995): 107–36.

Nelson, Stephanie A. *God and the Land: The Metaphysics of Farming in Hesiod and Vergil.* Oxford: Oxford University Press, 1998.

Niemeier, Wolf-Dietrich. "Greeks vs. Hittites: Why Troy Is Troy and the Trojan War Is Real." *Archaeology Odyssey* (July–August 2002): 24–35, 55–56.

Nilsson, Martin P. *Mycenaean Origin of Greek Mythology.* Berkeley and Los Angeles: University of California Press, 1932.

North, Douglass. "Economic Performance through Time." *American Economic Review* 84:3 (June 1994): 359–68. From a lecture delivered in Stockholm, Sweden, December 9, 1993, when North received the Alfred Nobel Memorial Prize in Economic Sciences. Published with permission of the Nobel Foundation.

Osborne, Robin. *Classical Landscape with Figures: The Ancient Greek City and Its Countryside.* Dobbs Ferry, NY: Sheridan House, 1987.

Palaima, Thomas. "Classics: Apocalypse Now or Working toward the Future?" *Classical Bulletin* 75:1 (1999): 85–97.

Papadopoulos, John K. "Phantom Euboeans." *Journal of Mediterranean Archaeology* 10:2 (December 1997): 191–219.

Papakonstantinou, Zinon. "Dancing Zeus: Leisure and Society in Archaic and Classical Greece." Ph.D. diss., University of Washington, submitted July 2003.

Parry, Adam, ed. *The Making of Homeric Verse: The Collected Papers of Milman Parry.* Oxford: Clarendon Press, 1971.

Parry, M., A. B. Lord, and D. E. Bynum. *Serbo Croatian Heroic Songs.* Collected by Milman Parry. Vol. 3. Cambridge: Harvard University Press, 1974.

Pietsch, C. *Die Argonautika des Apollonios von Rhodes.* Hermes Einzelschriften 80. Stuttgart: Franz Steiner Verlag, 1999.

Pinker, Steven. *The Blank Slate: The Modern Denial of Human Nature.* New York: Viking, 2002.

Popham, M. R., L. H. Sackett, and P. G. Themelis, eds. *Lefkandi I: The Iron Age.* London: Thames and Hudson, 1980.

Powell, Barry. *Homer and the Origin of the Greek Alphabet.* Cambridge: Cambridge University Press, 1991.

Pritchett, W. K. *Studies in Ancient Greek Topography.* Vol. 1. Berkeley and Los Angeles: University of California Press, 1965.

Pucci, P. "Banter and Banquets for Heroic Death." In *Post-structuralist Classics,* ed. A. Benjamin, 132–59. New York: Routledge, 1988.

Rainbird, C. Paul. "Islands Out of Time: Towards a Critique of Island Archaeology." *Journal of Mediterranean Archaeology* 12:2 (1999): 216–34.

Rapp, G., and J. A. Gifford, eds. *Troy: The Archeological Geology.* Supp. monograph 4. Princeton: Princeton University Press, 1982.

Rehm, A. "Griechische Kalendar. III." *Sitzungsberichte der Heidelberger Akademie der Wissenschaften. Philosophisch-historische Klasse* 3:3 (1913).

Renfrew, Colin. *The Emergence of Civilisation: The Cyclades and the Aegean in the Third Millennium B.C.* London: Methuen, 1972.

———. "Explanation Revisited." In *Theory and Explanation in Archaeology,* ed. Colin Renfrew, Michael J. Rowlands, and Barbara Abbott Segraves, 5–23. New York: Academic Press, 1982.

Richards, Martin, et al. "Tracing European Founder Lineages in the Near Eastern mtDNA Pool." *American Journal of Human Genetics* 67 (2000): 1251–76.

Rieu, E. V., trans. *The Voyage of Argo.* By Apollonius of Rhodes. Harmondsworth: Penguin Books, 1967.

Robb, Kevin. *Literacy and Paideia in Ancient Greece.* New York: Oxford University Press, 1994.

Rose, Mark. Review of *Noah's Flood,* by William Ryan and Walter Pitman. *Archaeology* 52:1 (1999): 75–78.

Rowlands, M. J. "Processual Archaeology as Historical Social Science." In *Theory and Explanation in Archaeology,* ed. Colin Renfrew, Michael J. Rowlands, and Barbara Abbott Segraves, 155–74. New York: Academic Press, 1982.

Scodel, Ruth. "Poetic Authority and Oral Tradition in Hesiod and Pindar." In *Speaking Volumes: Orality and Literacy in the Greek and Roman World,* ed. Janet Watson, 109–37. Leiden: Brill, 2001.

Scott, Lionel. "Were There Polis Navies in Archaic Greece?" In *The Sea in Antiquity,* ed. G. J. Oliver, R. Brock, T. J. Cornell, and S. Hodkinson, 92–115. BAR International Series 899. Oxford: Hadrian Books, 2000.

Severin, Timothy. "Jason's Voyage: In Search of the Golden Fleece." *National Geographic* (September 1985): 406–20.

———. *The Jason Voyage: The Quest for the Golden Fleece.* London: Hutchinson, 1985.

Shanks, Michael. *Classical Archaeology of Greece.* New York: Routledge, 1996.

Shanks, Michael, and Christopher Tilley. *Re-constructing Archaeology: Theory and Practice.* 2d ed. New York: Routledge, 1992.

Simpson, Richard Hope. *Mycenaean Greece.* Park Ridge, NJ: Noyes Press, 1981.

Sinclair, T. A. *Hesiod: Works and Days.* Hildesheim, Germany: Georg Olms Verlagsbuchhandlung, 1932.

Sjöquist, K. E., and Paul Åstrom. *Pylos: Palmprints and Palmleaves.* Göteborg, Sweden: P. Åström, 1985.

Snodgrass, A. M. "The Site of Askra." In *La Béotie antique,* ed. G. Argoud and P. Roesch, 87–95. Paris: Éditions du Centre National de la Recherche Scientific, 1985.

Spathari, Else. *Sailing through Time: The Ship in Greek Art.* Athens: Kapon Editions, 1995.

Starr, Chester. *The Origins of Greek Civilization: 1100–750 B.C.* London: Jonathan Cape, 1962.

Stobart, J. C. *The Glory That Was Greece: A Survey of Hellenic Culture and Civilization.* London: Sidgwick and Jackson, 1911.

Tandy, David. *Warriors into Traders.* Berkeley and Los Angeles: University of California Press, 1997.

Taylor, Walter W. "A Study of Archeology." *Memoirs of the American Anthropological Association* 69 (1948). Reprinted in *American Anthropologist* 50:3, pt. 2 (1948): 95–96.

Theochares, Demetrios R. "Iolkos: Whence Sailed the Argonauts." *Archaeology* 11 (1958): 13–18.

Thomas, Carol G. "The Greek Age of Heroes: Myth Becomes History." *Historically Speaking* (September 2002): 6–8.

———. "Mycenaean Law in Its Oral Context." *Studi micenei ed egeoanatolici* 25 (1984): 247–53.

Thomas, Carol G., and Craig Conant. *From Citadel to City-State: The Transformation of Greece, 1200–700 B.C.E.* Bloomington: Indiana University Press, 1999.

Thomson, J. A. K. *Studies in the Odyssey.* Oxford: Clarendon Press, 1914.

Trachtenberg, Marc. "The Past under Siege." In *Reconstructing History: The Emergence of a New Historical Society,* ed. E. Fox-Genovese and E. Lasch-Quinn, 9–11. New York: Routledge, 1999. Originally published in *Wall Street Journal,* July 17, 1998.

Treister, Mikhail. "The Trojan Treasures: Description, Chronology, Historical Context." In *The Gold of Troy: Searching for Homer's Fabled City,* trans. Christine Sever and Mila Bonnichses and ed. Vladimir Tolstikov and Mikhail Treister, 197–234. New York: H. N. Abrams, 1996.

Vansina, Jan. *Oral Tradition as History.* Madison: University of Wisconsin Press, 1985.

Wade-Gery, H. T. *The Poet of the Iliad.* Cambridge: Cambridge University Press, 1952.

Wagstaff, J. M. "The New Archaeology and Geography." In *Landscape and Culture: Geographical and Archaeological Perspectives,* 26–36. Oxford: Blackwell, 1987.

Walcot, Peter. *Greek Peasants, Ancient and Modern.* Manchester: Manchester University Press, 1970.

———. *Hesiod and the Near East.* Cardiff: University of Wales Press, 1966.

Wallace, Paul. "Hesiod and the Valley of the Muses." *Greek, Roman, and Byzantine Studies* 15:1 (1974): 4–24.

Watson, Richard. "The 'New Archeology' of the 1960s." *Antiquity* 46 (1972): 210–15.

———. "What the New Archaeology Has Accomplished." *Current Anthropology* 21 (1991): 275–91.

Wedde, Michael. *Towards a Hermeneutics of Aegean Bronze Age Ship Imagery.* Peleus Band 6. Mannheim and Mohnesee: Bibliopolis, 2000.

West, M. L. *Hesiod: Works and Days.* Oxford: Clarendon Press, 1978.

Whitley, David S. "New Approaches to Old Problems: Archaeology in Search of an Ever Elusive Past." In *Reader in Archaeological Theory,* ed. David S. Whitley, 1–34. New York: Routledge, 1998.

Wiener, Malcolm. "The Isles of Crete? The Minoan Thalassocracy Revisited." In *Thera and the Aegean World,* vol. 3, pt. 1, pp. 128–60. London: Thera Foundation, 1990.

Wilson, David. *The New Archaeology.* New York: Alfred A. Knopf, 1974.

Windschuttle, Keith. *The Killing of History.* New York: Free Press, 1996.

Wolf, Friedrich A. *Prolegomena ad Homerum.* Berlin: S. Calvary Eiusque

Socium, 1876. Now available in English: Anthony Grafton, Glenn W. Most, and James E. G. Zetgel, *Prolegomena to Homer* (Princeton: Princeton University Press, 1985).

Woodward, Roger. *Greek Writing from Knossos to Homer: A Linguistic Interpretation of the Origin of the Greek Alphabet and the Continuity of Ancient Greek Literacy.* New York: Oxford University Press, 1997.

Wright, James C. "The Place of Troy among the Civilizations of the Bronze Age." In *The World of Troy: Homer, Schliemann, and the Treasures of Priam,* ed. Deborah Boedeker, 35–50. Washington, DC: Society for the Preservation of the Greek Heritage, 1997.

Zwingle, Erla. "Black Sea Coast: Crucible of the Gods." *National Geographic* 202:3 (September 2002): 74–101.

Index

Aegean: Bronze Age, 52, 56; regional context, 53–54
—archaeology: discovery of new sites, 52–53, 56; interdisciplinary nature of, 53; new technologies, 53; dating and chronology, 53, 54, 55; regional and survey, 53, 66–67; mentioned, 42, 61. *See also* Archaeography
—trade and navigation: Bronze Age, 60–61, 65, 82; Neolithic, 60, 82; Black Sea contacts, 65, 77–79, 82
Agamemnon, 53, 83
Agora and legal procedure, 124
Agriculture, 11, 101–3, 105, 115, 123. *See also* Boeotia; Hesiodic poetry: *Works and Days*
Alexandrian poetry, 50–51. *See also Argonautica*
Al Mina, 117n46
American Historical Association (AHA), 26–27
Amphidamas. *See* Hesiod
Anatolia, 11, 60, 61, 65, 88, 112
Antimachos. *See Argonautica*: early precursors
Apollonius of Rhodes, 50, 51, 52, 67, 82, 87
Archaeography: defined, 54; mentioned, 63, 77
Archaeology: quantity of evidence, 5, 52; interpretation of evidence, 5, 32, 43, 44, 47; limitations of evidence, 7, 47; systems theory, 9, 32; new technologies, 10, 12, 16, 32, 38, 46–47, 53, 63, 77, 86; and allied disciplines, 16, 43, 53; objects as texts, 20–21, 33, 44; alien-

ation of the past, 21, 54; new archaeology, 24, 30–32, 43, 54; dependence of ancient history, 32, 47; methodology, 32, 52; new subfields, 33; survey archaeology, 33, 44, 53, 58, 85, 97–98, 129, 130; postprocessual, 42; excavation, 52; object biography, 55; mentioned, 1–8 passim, 14, 30, 39. *See also* Archaeography; History, historiography; Human-centered sciences
Archaic Age. *See* Greece: Archaic Age
Archilochus, 114, 126. *See also* Hesiodic poetry: gnomic poetry
Ardymi, Sismani, Vasiliki. *See* Dimini: palace
Argo, Argonauts. *See* Jason
Argonautica: Hellenistic characteristics, 50–51, 87; treatise on navigation, 50–51; character development, 51; Ur-Argonautica, 52, 55–59, 72, 78, 84, 94, 110; early precursors, 67–68; mentioned, 49, 87. *See also* Apollonius of Rhodes; Navigation, seafaring
Aristotle, 107, 119
Askra: archaeology of, 97–99, 130; located by Strabo, 98; Hill of Pyrgaki, 98–99; dominated by Thespiai, 99, 121; and seafaring, 116, 120–21; mentioned, 91, 96, 103, 105, 106, 112, 113, 116, 124. *See also* Hesiodic poetry: *Works and Days*
Athena. *See* Jason: legend of: deities in
Athens: *agora,* 4; Bronze Age, 56; Archaic political development, 107; mentioned, 26, 59, 83, 98
Aulis, 100–101

147

Onomastics. *See* Philology: personal names ending in *-eus*

Oral tradition: oral epic, 69–70, 71–72, 130; communal memory and nonliteracy, 70, 84, 94, 110–11, 130; and myth, 84, 86; and history, 84–85, 86; Mycenaean origins, 85; conservative nature of, 85–86; Hesiodic poetry, 92, 93; Homeric poetry, 110; anonymous nature of, 110–11; mentioned, 68

Orchomenos, 53, 56. *See also* Schliemann, Heinrich

Parry, Milman, 69, 94n9, 111. *See also* Oral tradition

Peisistratos. *See Iliad*

Pelias, 59. *See also* Jason

Phaeacia, Phaeacians, 122, 124

Philology: new criticism, 30, 34–37; classics, 34, 37; new classics, 35; statistical analysis of texts, 35, 42; deconstruction, 35; relativism, 36; modeling, 36; Jason and the Argonauts, 67–75 passim; personal names ending in *-eus,* 72–75; mentioned, 77, 91. *See also* Human-centered sciences: text deconstruction; Linear B

Phocylides. *See* Hesiodic poetry: gnomic poetry

Phrygia, 97

Pindar, 67. *See also Argonautica:* early precursors

Pinker, Steven, 41. *See also* Genetics

Pithecoussai. *See* Italy: colonization

Polybius, 44. *See also* History, historiography: alienation of the past; Human-centered sciences: text deconstruction

Populus Project, 42, 43, 44

Pottery: clay analysis, 53, 59, 87; object biography, 55; ship representations, 61, 118–19; inscriptions on, 89; mentioned, 65

Propontis. *See* Black Sea: Bronze Age exploration; Bosporus; Navigation, seafaring: navigating the Black Sea; Trade: Black Sea; Troy, Trojan War: trade center

Pylos: Linear B texts, 55n9, 73, 86–87; ruled by Neleus and Nestor, 56, 73, 83; mentioned, 57, 72, 124

Renfrew, Colin, 9, 11, 39. *See also* Archaeology: systems theory

Rieu, E. V., 51n5. *See also* Apollonius of Rhodes

Robb, Kevin, 113. *See also* Writing, written texts

Rowlands, M. J., 44. *See also* Human-centered sciences: reaction against "new" disciplines

Saussure, Ferdinand de, 20. *See also* Human-centered sciences: linguistics

Schliemann, Heinrich: contextualization of evidence, 56; reliance on Homer, 83; mentioned, 52–53, 62. *See also* Mycenae; Troy, Trojan War

Scodel, Ruth, 90

Semonides. *See* Hesiodic poetry: gnomic poetry

Severin, Timothy. *See Jason Voyage, The*

Shanks, Michael, 33. *See also* Human-centered sciences: reaction against "new" disciplines

Ships and ship construction: Bronze Age, 60, 80, 86; Neolithic, 60; pictographic evidence, 60, 61, 79, 118–19, 130; shipwrecks, 66–67; pentaconter, 78, 79, 86, 118; sails and decking, 79, 118; Dark Age and Archaic, 118, 119; mentioned, 50. *See also Jason Voyage, The;* Navigation, sea-faring

Sicily: colonization, 117; mentioned, 61

Silver, Morris. *See* Ulu-Burun shipwreck

Solon. *See* Hesiodic poetry: gnomic poetry

Sparta. *See* Greece: eighth-century revolutions

Stillman, W. A. *See* Schliemann, Heinrich

Stone, Lawrence, 26. *See also* History, historiography: new history

Strabo. *See* Askra

Survey archaeology. *See* Archaeology

Symplegades (Clashing Rocks). *See* Jason

Tandy, David, 106, 112, 127. *See also* Hesiod: literacy of

Televantou, Christina. *See* Navigation, seafaring: Neolithic

Thebes: Linear B texts, 55n9, 86–87; mentioned, 56, 83, 96, 100

Theognis, 111, 114. *See also* Hesiodic poetry: gnomic poetry

Theogony. See Hesiodic poetry

WITHDRAWN